In his book, Frank Gallagher has captured all the drama and difficulties of operating in a violent war zone, post-Saddam Iraq. As head of my personal security detail, Mr. Gallagher vividly captures the tense and dangerous duty he and his dedicated colleagues from Blackwater carried out under the most trying circumstances. On a number of occasions, some of them revealed in this book, Gallagher and his team literally saved lives—mine and others—through their quick and professional reactions to danger. If you want a flavor of life in post-invasion Iraq, this is the book for you.

L. Paul Bremer III
Former Presidential Envoy to Iraq

THE
BREMER
DETAIL

TO:
Danielle De Benedicks,

All the best.

Thanks,

[signature]

THE BREMER DETAIL

PROTECTING THE MOST THREATENED MAN IN THE WORLD

A MEMOIR

FRANK GALLAGHER

Agent-in-Charge
The Bremer Security Team, Iraq

WITH JOHN M. DEL VECCHIO

Author of *The 13th Valley*

Copyright © 2014 by Frank Gallagher and John M. Del Vecchio

Cover photograph by Christina Estrada Teczar

Cover design by Neil Alexander Heacox

978-1-4976-4398-7

Published by Charlie Foxtrot Books, LLC
www.charliefoxtrotbooks.com

Distributed by Open Road Integrated Media, Inc.
345 Hudson Street
New York, NY 10014
www.openroadmedia.com

FOR MY MOTHER, FLORENCE CARROLL GALLAGHER

Widowed in her early forties with five kids (three sons, two daughters), my mother never quit. She always set the bar high, encouraging us to do all that we could and to do it to the best of our abilities. She is also the type of person whom you never asked a question of if you were afraid to hear the answer. You could always expect complete, total, brutal honesty. Of course, this ended up with all three of her sons carrying guns for a living: John (retired after twenty-seven years in U.S. Army Special Forces), Jim (retired after twenty years with NYPD, thirteen years in narcotics), and me. Since 11 September 2001, she has had one or more sons continually working in some of the worst parts of the world. Sometimes more than one of us was away at the same time. Known to my Connecticut friends as "Babe" and to my "Frankwater" (the call sign that I would eventually be given in Iraq) friends as "Mama G," she's a legend.

A frequent conversation that she and I have had:

Mom: Frank, do you remember your eighth-grade graduation?
Me: Yes, Mom.
Mom: What did Sister Ann say about the parable of the talents?
Me: I remember.
Mom: Well, are you ever going to write that book?
Me: Yes, Mom.
Mom: Well, I hope you finish it before I die.
Me: Yes, Mom, I will.

Well, Mom, here it is! Thanks for all the support. I love you.

THE
BREMER
DETAIL

PRELUDE

After the United States invaded Iraq in 2003, and before power was turned over to the Iraqi Interim Government (IIG) the following June, American ambassador L. Paul Bremer III ran the country. As administrator of the Coalition Provisional Authority, Ambassador Bremer—essentially president, prime minister, Congress, the Supreme Court, and chancellor of the treasury—ruled by decree. From his first controversial orders banning the Ba'ath Party and dismantling Iraq's previous military, insurgent groups threatened his life. The danger never slowed him down. Each day he made two, three, as many as eight trips outside the Green Zone into the violent, post-Saddam state to meet with members of the Iraqi Governing Council (IGC), to begin restructuring the economy, to assist in the development of a new constitution, to design the privatization of industry and national resources, or to prepare new departments and bureaus for the day the nation would again govern itself.

With such power, in such a hostile environment, the Secret Service soon declared him the most-threatened man in the world. Protecting him was my job. I had known him from earlier assignments, having spent eight years providing security for Dr. Henry Kissinger and for Ambassador Bremer when he was managing director of Kissinger and Associates.

But this was different. No civilian-led protective security detail (PSD) had ever been charged with shielding a titular head of state. Daily I got intelligence briefs basically saying, "Uh . . . not sure how to tell you this, but today you are all going to die."

But I'm getting ahead of myself. Let me back up to the beginning. This is my story, and the story of how a group of dedicated protection professionals managed to do something they never thought possible. My name is Frank Gallagher, and I was the agent-in-charge of The Bremer Detail.

THURSDAY, 21 JULY 2003

I woke at 0800 and began my daily coffee intake. I fed the dogs, read the newspaper, contemplated what time I would head to the gym. It was a bright summer morning. After working nearly nonstop for nine years, I was taking a few months off to recharge my batteries. My wife, Kim, was upstairs cleaning; and our daughters, Kelli, twenty, and Katherine, fourteen, were still asleep. Ah, youth! What time I would hit the gym was just about the toughest decision I planned to make all day. Let's see—go at 1400? 1500?

I could hear Kim vacuuming. As a school administrator she too had a summer break. The novelty of my being home had not yet worn off. She was used to the prolonged absences that were always a part of my work. The phone rang. When I was home, Kim was accustomed to the roughly forty calls I would get each day from my brothers in the executive protection world. She knew many of them by their voices. I heard her switch off the vacuum and answer. By her tone I guessed it was a voice she did not recognize. This was confirmed when she called down without mentioning a name.

I picked up the kitchen phone. "Hello."

"Frank? This is Brian from Blackwater." The voice was friendly yet terse. "We have an opening for a guy to go to

Iraq and help with the security for Ambassador Bremer. You interested?"

It took a few seconds for it to register. My heart began to race. I didn't realize how ready I was, or how much I needed such a call. I had been idle for six weeks and growing antsier by the day. I missed being busy. "Sure," I answered. "When?"

"We'll need you to come down here to North Carolina, knock the rust off your weapons skills, take a physical fitness test. Then we'd like you to deploy in August."

"I'm in," I said. "When do you want me down there?"

"How about ten days."

"Cool. See you then."

Adrenaline kicked in. I took a deep breath, high-fived myself. My fists jabbed the air. Blackwater, regarded as the most prestigious outfit among top security professionals, had just extended me an offer. I poured myself another cup of coffee. My mind was racing. How would I tell Kim and the kids?

At this stage of my career I never thought I'd be going to a war zone. In my Marine Corps days in the '80s, I went to Cuba, Africa, the Persian Gulf, and all over Europe, but, like many of my Recon brothers, never during wartime. We prepared, we went on deployments, we risked our lives during training and got as good as one could get, but we never got to play in the big game. Politics is tough! That ate at me, us. We had done our jobs, but time and circumstances had denied us the opportunity to fight for our country. It was hard to live with.

In the high-end security world the mystique of Blackwater attracted a lot of protection specialists. Many tried out, but only a few made the cut. To even be considered was an ego boost and a big-time thrill.

And the opportunity for me to work again with Ambassador Bremer was compelling. I had worked extensively with him during my years as director of security for former U.S. Secretary of State Henry A. Kissinger. Kissinger's geopolitical consulting firm was composed of elite specialists. Ambassador Bremer, former ambassador-at-large for counterterrorism and ambassador to the Netherlands, was a close colleague of Dr. Kissinger, and a key executive in the firm. He was extremely bright, disciplined, and had a great sense of humor.

The combination of the war zone, Blackwater, and Ambassador Bremer was simply an opportunity too good to pass up. So much had happened in the preceding two years—starting with the terror attacks on the World Trade Center. For me, this was also the culmination of those events. As the image of me heading to Iraq took hold my body and mind electrified. This was gonna be interesting. Little did I know.

11 September 2001, elicits strong emotions. Some mourn the loss of a single life; others grieve for the hundreds of courageous men and women who were simply doing their job that crisp, clear morning. For many it is the sheer magnitude of more than three thousand deaths. The attacks didn't happen in some foreign land whose name most Americans can't spell and can't find on a map. They happened here. In our own backyard! In our country!

Within hours of the fireballs and crumbling towers the feeling of being untouchable, regardless of what was happening in far-off corners of the world, was reduced to rubble. The safety and security to which an entire generation had grown accustomed, even perhaps entitled, was stripped away, replaced to varying degrees by fear, anger, and a vocal demand for retribution.

As a former Recon Marine I readily admit retribution was something I took for granted. Not that I had any notion it would be mine to dispense. Those days had long passed, and, quite honestly, my chosen career placed a significant emphasis on avoiding the sort of risks that are commonplace on the battlefield. But I did not doubt retribution would be dispensed in response to the attacks, nor that when the time was right that we would do it. Our armed forces are the best in the world; the men and women who serve in them are the most capable on the planet. Period. End of story.

I'm ill equipped to debate the decisions that were made at the time by President Bush. It was his responsibility to make the decisions he felt were in the best interests of the nation. What I will say is I wholeheartedly supported them. More important, I'm glad they were his to make, not mine.

Soon after the September 11 attacks, the United States invaded Afghanistan, followed shortly thereafter by the invasion of Iraq. We were now fighting two wars in two countries, a scenario around which our entire military strategy was based. As often happens in the real world, the two-war doctrine barely survived first contact. It quickly became apparent we simply weren't prepared for the complexities of fighting simultaneous *asymmetrical* wars. These are conflicts where a small, poorly organized or poorly equipped adversary has an advantage over more conventional forces due to terrain, population, and initiative. The generals found holes in our preparation that needed filling. That's where guys like me came in—but again I'm getting ahead of myself.

I can't say I was surprised at how events unfolded, but I found it maddeningly frustrating. I had grown up in a military unit where the typical operating assumption was the adversary, even if ill equipped, ill trained, and poorly led, would have the tactical advantage of operating on his own turf. In my civilian career as a protection specialist (more commonly referred to as a bodyguard) I recognized that regardless of the resources you have at your disposal, the bad guy has the advantage of deciding when and how to attack. We play defense and try to make it as tough as possible for them to succeed. Someone far smarter than me once wrote "we hold these truths to be self-evident," and in my little slice of the world the truths that were self-evident tended to be both simple and straightforward. Right at the top of that list was the fact that, regardless of how much money, how many guns, or how many lawyers you have, a small handful of bad guys armed with superior knowledge of the terrain, enough time to plan, and a little ingenuity will, given the opportunity, kick your ass around the block every day of the week and twice on Sundays. And they're more than happy to do so without the benefit of shiny new, high-tech weaponry, slick tactical clothing, or cool sunglasses. From the outside looking in, there was little doubt the U.S. military was learning this lesson the hard way; and, like most lessons learned the hard way, it was painful, embarrassing, and costly.

But learn they did. It didn't take long for forward-thinking military leaders to understand the challenges they faced and to come up with viable solutions. They recognized that the decades of recruiting and investing in smarter, more capable troops could and would only pay dividends if these troops could be brought to bear on the enemy. This meant freeing up troops from mundane, behind-the-scenes tasks that drive the military's war machine; and rethinking how units could best utilize their most precious resource—their people. Although I am not sure what the ratio is these days, back when I served it was generally accepted that for every Marine, soldier, airman, and sailor serving in a combat role, seventeen were serving in support. So rethinking and reshaping how we go to war was by no means a small undertaking.

As the military adapted to the new reality in Afghanistan and Iraq, it recognized the urgent need to fill all the vacant positions created by moving troops to more critical, combat-oriented missions. It also recognized that the traditional fallback plan, the use of Reserve and National Guard troops to fill those voids, wasn't going to work because entire Reserve and Guard units were already being prepped for deployment and would need all their personnel to perform their missions. Recruiting and training more people—a costly, time-consuming endeavor in the best of times—wasn't a viable option, either. But somewhere, someone recognized that there were, in fact, a substantial number of people in the private sector who had the skill sets needed to fill those positions. In fact, many of these folks had developed those skills while serving in the military. When all was said and done, the folks who matter recognized it would be more timely and cost-effective to contract the resources they needed as opposed to taking the traditional route of recruiting and training organic resources.

So, for the first time ever, this country saw the wide-scale deployment of civilian contractors working in a war zone quite literally alongside the military, performing jobs traditionally performed by military personnel. These contractors included cooks, truck drivers, administrative assistants, advisors, and, of course, security specialists. Regardless of their job, and not unlike the folks who Tom Brokaw wrote about in his bestselling book *The Greatest Generation,* every single one of these people was willing to step up, make tremendous sacrifices, and assume tremendous risks despite having no retirement benefits, limited health coverage, absolutely no guarantees of continued employment, no unions to negotiate on their behalf for better working conditions, or most of the other things the typical American worker takes for granted. And in doing so, these civilians enabled the military to function more efficiently and effectively.

Thousands of civilian contractors have been injured or killed, yet when all was said and done there were no celebrations, no parades when they came home. Hell, they were lucky to get a paragraph in the local newspaper. More often they were criticized or demonized by people who knew nothing about what they had done or the sacrifices they had made. In my mind the overwhelming majority of these people are heroes in the same sense that the military people they served besides are heroes. No one forced them to go somewhere or do something they did not want to. They went because they felt a duty to this country.

They knew the risks and despite them, because they believed they could contribute something to the effort, they chose to put themselves in harm's way.

Don't get me wrong. Patriotism certainly wasn't the only factor that played into the decision made by many. The pay was good and the promise of adventure was appealing. Now I recognize that to the average person this line of thinking is, at best, foreign, perhaps bizarre. "Average" people—those who make up more than 90 percent of the population—go through life attempting to avoid confrontation at just about every opportunity and at almost any cost. A certain segment of the population counts on this. They are the criminals and evildoers, and they are quick to prey on those who are willing to take abuse, accept injustice, or just look the other way in order to avoid confrontation. I can't speak for the cooks, administrative assistants, or truck drivers, but I can tell you that security contractors tend to fall into a third category—one made up of the 1 percent of the population willing to stand up to criminals and others who prey on the innocent. In a different place and time they were cops, soldiers, and "protection specialists" or in layperson's terms, bodyguards. They were motivated by all those things already mentioned—patriotism, adventure, a decent paycheck—but most of all they were motivated by the understanding that most people in the world need protection, and that they are the ones who can provide it.

I'm not sure how psychiatrists, psychologists, politicians, or pundits might view this profession today, but I do know that for thousands of years those who chose to protect others, to serve as bodyguards, were viewed honorably and treated with respect.

It wasn't until professional protectors answered the call to ply their trade in a war zone that they became looked down upon and were called mercenaries and thugs. I am not sure how the hell that happened, but I can tell you that it couldn't be further from the truth. I say this because I have been a protection specialist for more than twenty years and have worked as a security contractor.

I have more than a few reasons for writing this book, some of which are easy to articulate, others not so much. One reason is the desire to provide a realistic portrayal of the work that security contractors did, day in and day out, in Iraq. Not some sensationalized story, but the unvarnished truth. Another reason is a desire to provide some insight into the courage and sacrifice that many of those contractors made to accomplish the extraordinarily difficult and very noble mission of keeping others alive in a country torn apart by war, by decades of strife wrought by an evil dictator, and by a general distrust of Western governments. But mostly I am writing this book to dispel the myths and misconceptions about who these security contractors were. Unlike the rest of the world I know them firsthand. I know them to be hardworking men trying to earn an honest living in the face of tremendous personal risk, confusing and conflicting directives, and competing political agendas.

Right up front I will tell you that the company I worked for was Blackwater, a company that was ultimately brought down by the tragic events that occurred on 16 September 2007, in Nisoor Square, a place few Americans outside of Iraq even knew existed. To be clear on this, I was not in Nisoor Square that day, nor did

I know any of the contractors involved in what would become one of the most highly publicized, controversial events involving security contractors. For those who may not be familiar with the incident, on that day a Blackwater convoy was moving through the square when it reported taking fire and, in turn, fired back. By the time the media coverage died down, the contractors, and the company itself, stood accused of killing seventeen innocent Iraqi men, women, and children, Blackwater's reputation was in tatters, and criminal charges were brought against some of members of the team. At the time I write this one man pled guilty to charges of manslaughter and agreed to testify against other members of the team. He is in prison. The charges against the others were initially dropped, but the men were once again charged in early 2014 and are expected to go to trail in June 2014. Blackwater no longer exists, and security contractors are generally painted with a broad brush of contempt, even by some in the protection profession.

In 2003, when I received my phone call, Blackwater was in its infancy. The idea of using private security contractors to protect American officials was nascent. I believe Erik Prince, founder of Blackwater, should be applauded for his willingness to step up and take the monumental risk of supporting the U.S. military and diplomatic efforts in Iraq and Afghanistan. At the time he accepted this first-of-its-kind contract to protect the highest-ranking U.S. official in a war zone, the rewards and risks were crystal clear: *Succeed in keeping Ambassador Bremer alive, and your company will have accomplished something no private company has ever achieved before. However, if Bremer gets killed, your company will serve as a poster child for those who believe a private company cannot possibly provide the level of protection required to safeguard government officials. Oh, and by the way, your company will, in all likelihood, never receive another government contract.*

But again, let me back up. This is my story and the story of how a group of dedicated protection professionals managed to do something that they themselves never thought possible.

21 JULY 2003

As I hung up and reached for my coffee, I heard Kim turn off the vacuum. She walked into the kitchen and asked who called. Deep breath: I told her it was Blackwater asking me if I wanted to work, and that I would be leaving for Iraq in three weeks. She clamped her teeth and did not say a word, obviously not overjoyed with the idea. Neither were my daughters (one in high school, one in college) when I told them. I explained it was only for thirty days, so it would be easy. I really believed this when I said it.

For the majority of my executive protection career I have kept well-known, recognizable figures safe. I have always had an excellent sense of the who, the where, and the when of potential problems. I've worked in forty-two different countries but never in a war zone environment. And I always came back safe. Africa, the Middle East, Europe, Asia—most spots were civilized, no spot had thousands of folks trying to kill my protectee. I expected Iraq to be similar. Boy, was I naïve as hell!

At age forty-four I was not in the same shape I was back when I was a Recon Marine. From talking to some of my friends, I knew Blackwater's physical fitness test would include a 1.5 mile run and some pull-ups. The pull-ups would be easy. The run? Yeah, not so much. I knew, too, I would have to get to the shooting range and put some holes in some targets to make sure I did not embarrass myself. So I made the decision to increase the tempo of my workouts and actually start running. I hate running.

In 2003 Blackwater, virtually unknown to the public, had a mystique of excellence and elitism among security specialists; and a reputation for hiring only the "best of the best." I was honored and nervous. I knew my friend Brutus had put my name in for consideration, and the last thing I wanted to do was make him look bad. In our world, if you recommend someone and he doesn't work out, you run the risk of getting fired for making a bad recommendation. Brutus was a great friend and a brother Recon Marine, and I certainly didn't want to sully his reputation. We had worked together for Dr. Kissinger for five years, and I knew Brutus thought I could do it or he would not have risked the recommendation. He had never bullshitted me.

I called Brutus and gave him the news. He had been working in Iraq for Blackwater for several months on a different project, and he cautioned me that the selection process was no joke. He gave me the limited insight he had about the upcoming project. We talked about the heat and the operations that were going on over there in the "sandbox." Iraq at this time was not going through the troubles that would soon begin. Coalition forces had been there for four months. The Iraqis still weren't quite sure what to expect as we attempted to convert the country from Saddam Hussein's dictatorship to a functioning democracy. The coalition was extremely hopeful the transition would be relatively painless. Insurgent attacks were not yet an everyday occurrence. This would soon change.

For the time being Americans seemed to be regarded as semiheroes for ousting Saddam, and there was general goodwill toward us. Brutus wished me good luck and gave me a list of things he thought would make my life somewhat easier. There were many things that could be purchased in Baghdad, but the main items that were always in short supply included: soap, deodorant, shoelaces, extra sunglasses, watch batteries, and Febreze. The Febreze was a key and essential part of the equipment load as the heat and all too frequent water outages could cause a man and his equipment to smell worse than the local dump. I couldn't admit it to him because of bro-rules, but I was nervous as hell. We laughed and I told him I would see him soon. At least, I hoped I would.

Trying out for anything has always been disconcerting to me. I knew from word of mouth that Blackwater was mainly staffed by former SEALs who had extensive special operations experience. Most had considerable time with DEVGRU (SEAL Team 6). I was a former Recon Marine, had been out for almost twenty years, and had been doing executive protection for most of that time—meaning suits and ties and flying around on private jets.

No body armor, no rifles. I knew Brutus had navigated through the Blackwater on-boarding process so I felt confident that, despite the sometimes intense interservice rivalry between the Recon guys and the SEALs, the SEAL team guys would give me a fair chance. I also knew they had called me because of my previous relationship with Ambassador Bremer. Blackwater was relatively new to the executive protection game, so I had that going for me.

Later that same afternoon I went to the gun store and bought a couple hundred rounds of ammo, then went to the range. The shooting went well, but I was fully aware of the fact that the guys who would be evaluating me were going to be shit hot shooters. I made a mental note that I would need at least a few more range sessions before I felt comfortable with my skill level. My accuracy was good, but my speed was not. Muscle memory would need to be reinvigorated. One thing to note about guys like us—former military, former cops, or as we say to each other "former action guys" (FAGs for short)—is we know and readily acknowledge where our weaknesses lie, and we actually try to get them up to par before a tryout. Yes, we work at it. Yes, we practice. Shooting is a perishable skill. If you don't practice, you don't shoot well. I didn't have access to an M-4 rifle so I was going to have to fire the thing cold and hope my hand-eye coordination would translate from handguns and my muscle memory for a carbine would come back quickly.

After addressing the weapons part of the tryout equation, I turned my attention to the run. One and a half miles in twelve minutes. Back in the day most of us could probably walk this fast, but this was not back in the day. Onslow Beach, the home of 2d Recon Battalion, was a distant memory. Even there, running had been a challenge for me. The USMC physical fitness test has a three-mile run, and to get maximum points the course had to be covered in eighteen minutes or less. My best time ever had been 19:10, and that had been at the end of Amphibious Reconnaissance School (ARS) when I was in my all-time peak condition. ARS was the school that Marines had to complete to get the military occupation specialty of 0321—Reconnaissance Man. I was lucky enough to go through the very first ARS course. It combined the most challenging physical aspects of U.S. Army Ranger School with the SEALs' Basic Underwater Demolition School (BUDS). Even after ARS, I could not max the run.

So I took my car out and mapped a 1.5-mile course around my neighborhood. I figured within ten days I should certainly regain some semblance of running shape. Next it was off to the running store to get a pair of shoes that would be up to the task. Apparently running shoes had evolved into highly specialized designs tailored to weight, stride length, and so on. At my weight, about 210, I was considered a Clydesdale not a thoroughbred and was thus directed toward a small rear corner of the store where a running shoe guru shepherded me through my purchase. And, of course, I bought some decent socks. A man has got to have decent socks.

I went home, put on my new shoes, and headed out the door. Apparently at age forty-four you really should stretch a bit before running for the first time in ten years. But, in my mind, tigers don't stretch; we just run out and kill things. I made it almost a hundred yards before I felt an intense pain shooting up my left leg. I (barely) hobbled back to the house, fully convinced I had torn my Achilles tendon. I made it to the kitchen and immediately started icing the injured area. It hurt like hell! This was not good.

Kim got home from the beach, saw the ice pack on my leg and the bottle of Motrin on the table, and casually asked what I had done. She was somewhat used to the periodic injuries her husband got because he refused to admit he was not twenty-one anymore. Trying to be stoic, I asked her if she would drive me to the orthopedic surgeon so I could figure out exactly how badly I was hurt. She picked up her keys and off we went. I was in extreme pain but was trying to be flippant. If she had not been there, I almost certainly would not have been able to drive myself. As we drove, a hundred scenarios played out in my mind. Complete tear. Rupture. Blackwater. Iraq. Let Brutus down. What was I going to do? How could this have happen? WTF?

The doctor examined it, took some x-rays, said I had only sprained, not torn, my Achilles.

Good. I asked about recovery time and chances for reinjuring it. He said this type of sprain usually took about two months to heal. TWO MONTHS????! I had nine days before the running and shooting events were to take place. He said to rest it, ice it, stay off it, and if I wanted, I could see a physical therapist. After I explained my upcoming deployment and schedule, he gave me some heavy-duty anti-inflammatories, made some calls, and got me into a physical therapist later that afternoon. I was beside myself with doubts.

The physical therapist started immediately with electrical stimulation and massage. He repeated the "rest, ice, elevation, and stay off it" advice. Yeah, like there was any chance this was going to happen! Instead of running I decided the next best thing was to try walking as far and as fast as I could. Kim was supportive and came with me. She only called me a pussy a few times. It was all I could do not to think about the position I found myself in. My ankle and leg hurt like hell.

I continued the meds and PT every day and started to feel a little better, but the specter of the run was hanging over my head like the grim reaper. And more than a few people thought the injury was a good thing as it would likely keep me from going through with the deployment. These folks clearly did not know me as well as they thought they did. My sole driver was my intention to go, to try out and do the absolute best I was capable of doing. Failure was not an option. Still, I must confess to a nagging worry that I would struggle, that I would not be able to force my way through the pain.

Blackwater called and set up my travel plans. I didn't mention the injury. We talked about the pay and the length of the contract. They wanted me to go for thirty days and were going to pay me $600 a day. I quickly did the math, thought 18K was a ton of money, and honestly figured it would be a cakewalk. Study long, study wrong.

Blackwater's original contract to keep Ambassador Bremer safe was to supply two men to supplement a protection team supplied by the U.S. Army's Criminal Investigative Division. I found this odd: two civilian contractors working alongside, for, and with regular U.S. Army personnel. But who was I to question anything? I would go and do the best I could and be home in a month. The whole thing was simply overwhelming. These were the days long before the contracting craze hit the sandbox. Blackwater had two guys with the ambassador and another thirty (The Dirty 30) working on another project. They had a total of thirty-two elite guys there, truly a far cry from the eventual thousands of contractors who would be working there a few years later. (By early 2005 Blackwater alone had approximately one thousand contractors in Iraq.)

MOYOCK, NC

The day arrived for me to head down to Moyock, North Carolina, for the big events—two days of nerve-wracking man tests. As luck would have it, somehow, in my state of confusion over the injury and the rehab, I screwed up the date. I thought I was flying on Monday. The plane ticket they sent was for Sunday. Imagine my horror when the phone rang Monday morning and Susan M. asked me if I had changed my mind about coming down. I had no idea what she was talking about. I quickly packed my bags, jumped in my car, and began the ten-hour drive to Moyock. The entire drive now consisted of me kicking myself in the ass for (a) not reading the itinerary that had been sent; (b) my injury; and (c) the great first impression I must have been making by proving reading comprehension was apparently not a strong part of my intellectual repertoire. I was beside myself. Ten hours is a long time to question and punish one's self.

I got there after dark. Following the instructions I had been given, I punched in the access control numbers to the main entrance gate and headed to the bunkhouse to try to get some sleep . . . like that was even remotely possible. The bunkhouse was half filled with folks there for different training courses. Like all men, we grunted acknowledgments but never exchanged any conversation. My room consisted of two bunk beds and a desk. Fortunately I was the only one in the room. I set my alarm for 0600 and tried to sleep. Brutus called from the sandbox, and I explained my fuckup to him and he laughed and reminded me that stuff like this happens with the SEALs all the time and not to sweat it. Easier said than done.

The next morning I went to the chow hall and had a couple of cups of coffee while I was trying to figure out who was who and where I should I go. August in NC is the closest thing to Africa-hot I have ever experienced. The flashbacks to Camp Lejeune and Onslow Beach were surreal. It was 90 degrees and 90 percent humidity. It was HOT. Truly uncomfortable.

I finally met up with Brian B and Susan M and they explained the day's events. I would head to the range with Steve Babs (former SEAL and weapons instructor) and shoot the Glock pistol that I was to be issued in Iraq, and an M-4 rifle. Did I say it was hot? I was already sweating through my clothes. Steve Babs and I went to the armory and grabbed a couple of pistols and rifles and several thousand rounds of ammo. Several thousand! I thought at first he was trying to intimidate me. Who shoots this much ammo in one day? Blackwater, that's who.

Babs was around thirty and in great shape. I was forty-four and in not-so-great shape. I put on the body armor (thirty pounds or so), the Glock pistol and spare magazines, and six magazines of M-4 ammunition. We went through a series of pistol fundamentals and then began shooting. And we shot, and we shot, and we shot, and we shot. From the holster. From a knee. From a prone position. From behind barricades. Did I say it was hot? I was drenched in sweat. Steve had a lot of water, and I drank as much as I could. Fainting would not have been a good thing. We then started moving and shooting. And running and shooting. My hands were sore from loading magazines. Then we shot moving targets. Then we shot more targets. And so it went until lunchtime.

After lunch, we picked up with the M-4. First the fundamentals and the basics. Once again, with about forty pounds of gear attached to my frame, we began shooting. From the standing position, from a knee, from a prone position. Behind barricades. Did I mention the heat? By now it was 100 degrees and we were in the sun. I was not sure if I'd make it through the afternoon. Finally around 1630 hours Babs called it a day. I must have done okay as he said he would see me tomorrow at the armory at 0800. I crawled back to the bunkhouse. My leg was on fire. My ass was chapped from the sweat that had dripped down my ass crack all day. My whole body was drained. My hands were bleeding from the thousands of rounds we had loaded. Brutus had been correct: Blackwater did not fuck around when it came to training.

The next morning the training continued. We moved on to rifle and pistol drills. We shot, and we shot, and we shot. Around 1000 hours Brian B came over and asked me to come to the office and talk with B-Town, who had been one of the first two guys on The Bremer Detail in Iraq. B-Town was a retired SEAL who had served over twenty years in the Teams. He explained how the detail was being run, and what I could expect. At first I thought he was kidding, but I quickly realized this was going to be way more real, and far more dangerous, than my experiences doing protection stateside. B-Town explained the group dynamics. We would *not* be working with Special Forces–caliber folks as I had hoped. The majority of the current detail was made up of reservists who had been called to active duty, and B-Town said they were not pleased to be working with contractors. *Great,* I thought. B-Town talked about the motorcade convoys and the advances, and the living conditions and the heat. It really was a great brief and I will be eternally grateful for his honesty.

Back to the range where Steve Babs continued to torture me with more and more complex shooting drills. My fingers were raw and bleeding from the nonstop reloading, but I said nothing and kept going. Finally, lunchtime came. I drank as much Gatorade as I could and crawled back to the bunkhouse to ice my leg. The damn run was scheduled for the next morning and, quite honestly, the shooting was sapping my energy levels.

Again back to the range. We shot for about an hour when Steve called a time-out. As we were walking toward the targets to examine them Babs pointed at a dragonfly buzzing around about seven yards in front of us. He laughed and said watch this. He drew his pistol and shot the dragonfly while it was in the air moving away from us and to the left—a truly awesome display of pistol marksmanship. The guy could shoot.

We talked about what we had done over the last few days, and he said he was satisfied and I was "good to go." We went to see Brian B and Babs gave me the thumbs-up. I was ecstatic. It was the most intense shooting session I had ever been through. Now only the run lurked in the back of my mind.

Brian B talked about the deployment dates. I read and signed the contract. We talked about life insurance, what would happen if we got involved in a shooting, and so on. I gave them my passport so they could get me a visa for Kuwait. Kuwait was the mustering site for folks heading to Iraq. They gave me a departure date and we shook hands. I walked out of the office with Babs and he took me to the spot where they issued gear. I got some shirts, trousers. He asked if I had any other questions and I said no. We shook hands and he wished me luck. He said it was over and to have a good trip home. I hesitated for a second and then asked about the physical fitness test. He said not to worry about it as the range had tested all he had needed to see. He said again I was "good to go." I thanked the sweet little baby Jesus in my own way. I grabbed my new "cool guy" gear and went back to the bunkhouse to pack my shit and escape before anybody could change their minds. I did not relax until I hit Delaware.

The drive home was, to say the least, interesting. The Northeast power grid had failed and a massive outage blacked out New York and the New England states. Traffic lights were out; toll booths and gas stations were closed. As I cruised through Delaware I heard radio reports of what was coming, so I gassed up and plotted how I could best get to Connecticut. I crossed into New Jersey. The drive became treacherous. About forty miles into the Garden State I began a laborious trek on nontoll roads. They too were jammed. Tempers were flaring. Drivers dove into small gaps in traffic like WW II kamikaze pilots attacking carriers. Finally the radio reported all the tolls on the Garden State Parkway had been opened to let traffic flow. I maneuvered back to the highway and had clear sailing to the Tappan Zee Bridge. The trip took six hours longer than it should have, but I was happy to be back in Connecticut. I thought, *If I don't get killed driving home, Iraq will be a cakewalk.*

I arrived home at about 0400. We had no power. I told Kim by candlelight that I had passed and would be leaving in two weeks. I told the girls the next morning. I hoped in a weird way they were happy for me, but I could sense concern on their faces. They were used to my disappearances, but it was usually to Paris or London or Australia or South America, not to a war zone. And definitely not to Iraq. Friends, too, questioned my sanity. The only thing I could say was that I had signed up to go, I would honor my commitment, and I would be home in a month. I was excited!

AUGUST 2003

Departure day arrived, and off I went to JFK with all the gear I thought I might need. Actually with way more than I would ever need. Since we were protecting the presidential envoy, I packed a couple of suits, some Polo shirts, ties, dress shoes, and a sport coat. And my cool-guy tactical gear. Little did I know I would need a lot more tactical, and a lot less executive, equipment.

Travel always has its travails. When I reached the counter of the American immigration line in Kuwait, I was directed to a room and told to take a seat. Behind the glass partition I could see the immigration officers drinking tea and smoking cigarettes. My passport rested on the table in front of them. After twenty minutes I knocked on the glass to see if there was a problem and was curtly told to sit back down. Thirty minutes later I knocked again. Once more I was told to sit. No one had even opened my passport. An hour later the "coffee break" ended and they stamped my passport. Welcome to Middle East time. The Kuwaitis apparently had forgotten how the United States had saved their asses during the first Gulf War. This cultural difference would end up being a pain in my ass more than a few times.

I retrieved my bags and went to look for the driver who was supposed to be waiting to take me to the hotel where I was to stay the first evening. No driver. Instead I found a shuttle bus. At the hotel front desk I was told there was no room for me. I explained I was transiting to Iraq, and they directed me to the other side where contractors registered. My name was on the manifest for the next morning, so they assigned me a bed. This was not quite the hotel room I hoped for. It had four beds, no locks on the doors, no TV, no phone, and only a single desk and chair. I dropped my gear and went to find a phone to tell the family I had arrived; and to phone Big Bird, the man who would become my partner in Baghdad.

Bird was a retired Army Delta guy. I got him on the phone and told him I would arrive the next day around midafternoon. He said he and Brett H would be there to pick me up. Brett was a former SEAL. Bird also told me that Bremer was in the United States for the next few days so we'd have time to go over everything before he returned. Cool, I thought. A good chance to reset the body clock and get used to the heat before we started working.

Next morning at 0400 I got on the bus for the airport. When we arrived our gear was placed on pallets, and we were told we'd have to wait for the plane to arrive to take us into Iraq. The pallets were loaded with everything from military-issue seabags and rucksacks to red women's suitcases. We were directed to a large military tent and told we would be called when they were ready for us. We waited. It was hot as hell. We waited some more. There was a nervous buzz of mindless chatter between the men and women who were waiting with me. You could see and feel the anticipation within the folks getting ready to fly into the war zone. I sucked down a few bottles of water; tried to stay calm.

Finally we boarded a U.S. Air Force C-130 filled with Americans—civilians and military. I could read anxiety on many faces. Some of the folk were just kids in their early twenties going to work for nongovernment organizations (NGOs). Some were military vets returning to their units.

The plane landed in Mosul. With engines still running the crew chief began to herd everyone off the plane and commanded us to keep walking until the pain stopped. I had no idea what he was talking about. Once off the plane I realized he was talking about the heat. It was 125 degrees outside, and combined with the heat from the engines it must have been 150 degrees. I thought I had taken the plane to hell. We had an hour to kill. You can talk about dry heat all you want, this was painfully hot. Like standing-in-front-of-a-giant-hair-dryer hot. It hurt to breathe. The crew began refueling, unloading gear, and loading additional cargo for the folks headed to Baghdad. I kept walking but there was no relief. We were directed to another tent and told we'd be called when the plane was ready. I downed two more bottles of water.

We off-loaded in Baghdad. Our gear had been placed on a number of pallets that forklifts had picked up and dropped off in the "baggage claim" area. If your stuff was on the bottom, you had to wait for the folks whose stuff was on top to grab theirs before you could get yours. I looked for Bird and Brett. There were two guys who looked as though they might be looking for me. I was correct. I threw my stuff in the back of their Suburban, and Bird handed me a rifle, a pistol, ammo, and a set of body armor. Then they told me what we would do if we were attacked. What had I signed up for?!

We raced down Baghdad International Airport Road (BIAP Road or "Route Irish" to the military in the area) at 70 mph.

Speed limits were nonexistent and speed was your biggest ally as you drove the gauntlet. Burned-out vehicles littered the roadside. Bird and Brett explained some of the tactics the insurgents were using to attack coalition forces: dropping grenades off overpasses onto oncoming traffic; pulling up alongside vehicles and firing at them with AK-47s; planting improvised explosive devices (IEDs) in animal carcasses. The bad guys knew no Iraqis would touch the rotting flesh, and they could wait for an American convoy to drive past before detonating the bomb. True to form the bad guys were not playing fair.

Brett said they had one stop to make in town before we went to Saddam's palace. His palace had been turned into the head-quarters for the Coalition Provisional Authority (CPA). We drove through downtown Baghdad and stopped at a storefront. I was told to take a security position, to watch the car, and to be alert for people approaching. They went in and quickly came out with about ten cases of beer and several bottles of assorted adult beverages. I thought to myself I had just signed a document a few days earlier stating I wouldn't drink while I was in-country. I casually asked Bird about the drinking rules. He laughed like hell and said they had all signed the same document. This was the first time the "big boy" rule was explained to me—*We do what we want as long as it does not affect the mission or mission readiness.*

We arrived at a labyrinth of checkpoints and speed bumps buzzing with military personnel—the Green Zone. It was a secure area designed to keep the bad guys away from U.S. and coalition workers and officials as they charted the course for the future of Iraq. We went directly to my new home, a trailer that I would share with Bird. It had a toilet, shower, and sink area that we shared with two guys living in the other half of the trailer. Fortunately we also had a refrigerator, a perk B-Town had apparently "found." I unpacked while Bird drove Brett to the Al Rasheed Hotel. For his last few days in-country Brett had taken a room there to experience its luxury. For media and visitors the Al Rasheed, still open for business, offered the best accommodations in the Green Zone. Many Americans lived there. All this would soon change.

It was hot! The air-conditioning in the trailer could barely keep up. Bird returned and took me to the palace for my ID card and to introduce me to the army guys with whom we would be working.

To say my arrival was met with a look of disapproval would be an understatement. The Criminal Investigative Division (CID) guys who protect the secretary of defense and other high-ranking Defense Department personnel, did not like "dirty contractors." Bird filled me in as best he could about what the problems were and how to best make it work. He had previously been part of the contractor team that had worked on the Karzai detail in Afghanistan, and he had tried to get these CID guys to incorporate some of the tactics he had used successfully over there. There was a lot of pushback from these guys as they truly believed they knew what they were doing and were certain their ideas were always superior to any idea from a contractor. It was awkward at best. I met the staff who supported the ambassador. Most were young, enthusiastic government employees who had volunteered to be there and become part of history.

We went back to the trailer where I got a quick tutorial on the foot and driving formations the CID guys were using to try and keep Ambassador Bremer safe. I was told we also had to watch the office where Bremer worked, while the CID guys would watch his bedroom—an empty office redesigned as sleeping quarters. It had a cot, a desk, and a lamp—Spartan living at best.

I needed to know where the office was, the parking areas, the ambassador's living space, and anything and everything else that could and would impact the job we were doing. There was a lot to learn, including the priority of the moment—food. The chow hall was an immense crystal, marble, and gold room the size of two side-by-side football fields converted into an old-style high school cafeteria where several hundred folks could eat. We grabbed trays, some plastic utensils, and then waited in line to have the subcontracted third-country national spoon food of our choices onto a plate. Next we jockeyed for a place to sit at tables with the capacity for twenty or more people. As the U.S. presence had increased, there were so many people at the Coalition Provisional Authority (CPA) that overflow seating had to be added to accommodate the masses.

After chow we retreated to the trailer where we enjoyed a cold beer, then to the Al Rasheed Hotel to link up with Brett. At the Al Rasheed I was introduced to a bar that Saddam's sons had modeled after a '70s disco, Studio 54, I think. The lights of a twelve-foot-high Ba'ath Party symbol pulsated in the center of the dance floor. It was surreal. The place was mobbed with other contractors, U.S. military personnel, government employees. Bird took me around to introduce me to several of his friends.

The music was blasting, people were dancing, and you would never have known there was a raging conflict going on two hundred yards away. All in all, I was stunned by what I had seen on my first few hours in-country. We went back to the trailer and I crashed like a dead person.

The next morning the power was out and there was no running water. Bird explained this was a common occurrence, and the best way to shower was to use the outdoor shower at the pool or to jump in the palace pool. Bird took me to chow, then to the gym. He was a machine, a workout warrior. I was exhausted, but tried to keep up. I knew I had to do it or I'd never survive my month. Bird was scheduled to rotate out with me at the end of September.

After the gym the tour continued. It was extremely confusing as it appeared to me there was neither rhyme nor reason to how things had been laid out. Apparently groups had come into the palace and claimed space based upon the old first come, first claim rule. Again we met with our CID and other military counterparts. I still did not get a warm and fuzzy feeling from them. It seems as if there had been rumors wafting back to the State Department or maybe the White House that the army guys were not really up to the task of keeping Bremer safe. They were very defensive. Hell, I was just trying to fit in and become part of the team. I had no hidden agenda.

Within three days, their worst fears were confirmed. The U.S. Secret Service came into town with a four-man assessment team led by Jim Cawley. After analysis and observation, he declared Ambassador Bremer to now be the most-threatened man in the world; and that his protection would require a higher skill set than CID currently possessed. CID was severely ass hurt by his assessment.

About this time the ambassador came back to Iraq. We picked him up at the airport, loaded him onto a Black Hawk helo, and flew him to the Green Zone. He went directly to his office and to work. Ambassador Bremer never took time off. To watch him and his staff work was amazing. Eighteen-hour days were short days. He finally quit for the day, and when he got back to his room, I reintroduced myself to him. He seemed shocked to see me there, but I think he was happy to see a known and friendly face. Unfortunately, our army counterparts were less than thrilled with the fact the ambassador and I had a relationship that went back ten years. Their reaction to his reaction was priceless. Oh well.

Bird and I were called to a meeting with Jim Cawley from the Secret Service where we were told the CID guys were going to be replaced. At this time we didn't know by whom. The next day, 28 August 2003, we were told Blackwater would be taking over Bremer's protection; and based upon my work with Kissinger and my relationship with Bremer, Jim Cawley was going to recommend that I be named the agent-in-charge (AIC) of the detail. I had spent eight years traveling to dozens of countries with Dr. Kissinger and Ambassador Bremer and had experience with both the protocols of the Secret Service and the State Department. The CID guys were severely pissed off, but the reality is—despite all the posturing—somebody from the

Department of Defense and/or from the White House made the decision. The Secret Service did not make the decision; Blackwater did not make the decision; and I certainly didn't make the decision.

Blackwater headquarters called and asked if I would take the new position. What a roller-coaster ride these first days in-country had become. The thirty-day promise to Kim and the kids was on my mind. So was the mission. Yesterday I was one of two contractors working with Army CID; now I was being asked to run a thirty-six-man team. The shock was unbelievable. What had I signed up for? Nowhere in my mind had I imagined this scenario.

I told Blackwater, "Yes." Bird would become my shift leader. The Secret Service briefed Bremer. He agreed to the switch. My nerves were jangled; adrenaline pumped; we were off to the races!

Blackwater quickly found another thirty-four guys, gave them a quick train-up, and prepped to send them over to join Bird and me. The train-up consisted of weapons training and qualifications (Glock, M-4), a physical, a physical fitness test, a psychological evaluation, and some basics on the formations they thought we would be using. They had less than a week to staff the detail. It wasn't the best of situations, but Blackwater had agreed to undertake the mission and time was of the essence. Fortunately, Blackwater had the advantage of an elite reputation in the security community and could recruit good people. While this was going on security enhancements recommended by the Secret Service needed implementation, including reinforcing the ambassador's office to withstand explosions, and further restricting access to his office. We also had to find better, more secure living quarters for the boss—a house where he could live and that we could protect.

In addition to the thirty-four guys that were selected, Blackwater also told me that as part of the contract there would be three MD-530 helicopters, six pilots, and four mechanics joining us as soon as they could recruit the right guys and get the "Little Birds" outfitted and ready for Baghdad. Estimated time of arrival was "about" thirty days. Finding housing and a place for the Little Birds would be a problem in and of itself.

Bird and I were still working with the CID guys. It was not pretty. Hell hath no fury like a soldier being replaced by contractors. Somehow, to them, Bird and I were accountable for the changeover. They went out of their way to make our lives as difficult as possible. We pulled office watch all day long and made every Red Zone run with the boss. The CID totally slacked off. They used the office time to sleep, and at night they posted only one man outside the boss's room. It quickly caught up with them. Early one morning while the Secret Service team was there doing some assessment, the agents went to the ambassador's room and found no CID there. Another morning the ambassador left his room to find himself unprotected. Saying nothing he simply laced up his running shoes and went for his morning run without any security. From a protection perspective this was not good, not even if the ambassador enjoyed the solitude of being able to run alone for the first time in months.

The Secret Service agents explained to us that incidents like these were a big part of the reason that CID was being replaced. Jim Cawley warned Bird and me that we had better never let them happen on our watch.

We never did.

SEPTEMBER 2003—BOOTS ON THE GROUND

We got word our new guys would be inbound on 4 September. I was anxious for the official handover to take place, for it to be just our team, but first we had to find a place for them to live. The existing and functional trailers behind the palace were full, and the new ones in the five-hundred-man camp under construction were not yet ready. Our guys would be coming with communications equipment, weapons, ammo, two explosive-detection dogs, etc. We needed space. Bird somehow commandeered an old ballroom, and we placed thirty-four cots in it. Not the greatest living conditions by any stretch of the imagination, but certainly different. There was a small bathroom—complete with gold-plated fixtures—which all thirty-four guys would have to share. Organizing the logistics of the buildup while the ambassador worked his eighteen- to twenty-hour days required full concentration. The CID guys did not help us at all.

Once the Blackwater team arrived there was supposed to be a ninety-six-hour grace period where the transition from CID to Blackwater would take place. The CID guys were to give us all the maps, grid coordinates, and advance surveys they had done. Unfortunately, the animosity had reached a level where little information sharing occurred. And Secretary of Defense (SecDef) Donald Rumsfeld was also coming to town. The team needed to hit the ground running. We had one day to train as a unit, and we were then handed the responsibility of protecting the most-threatened man in the world! Not the smoothest way to handle it. But we made it work.

Our first Blackwater-only Red Zone meeting was a trip to the house of Abdul Aziz al-Hakim, a theologian and politician who was a member of the U.S.-appointed Iraqi Governing Council (IGC). The Red Zone was considered any part of Iraq not completely protected and controlled by the U.S. or coalition forces. I asked the CID guys for the address and the grid coordinates so we could plan the mission. They told me they did not have the information. I went to the ambassador's office and was told the ambassador had just been there a few weeks before and that CID had taken him there. Needless to say, once the staff of the ambassador got involved we suddenly had access to all the information we needed. It was childish and petty. This went on for weeks until we were eventually able to put together our own information database.

Setting up and running a protective security detail (PSD) team is more complicated than most people realize. From the outside people see a team around the protectee and think this is what is done. In reality there are many moving parts, and many decisions have been made prior to taking the protectee to the event. The guys around the protectee, known as the Detail, or Detail Team, are the face of the PSD, but behind the scenes, long before the protectee arrives at the venue, a world of planning and coordination has taken place.

And we were working with virtually unknown "raw material." Bird and I had the unenviable task of taking thirty-four men who had zero experience in the Baghdad environment and placing them in positions to keep Ambassador Bremer and our own team members alive. And we had twenty-four hours to do it. A cursory examination of their résumés, brief conversations, and talks with a few of the new guys we had known previously helped make the decisions, but at this point everything, every day, was a work in progress.

The key element to any PSD team, and the most important part of every mission, is the work done by the advance team. The advance team has the single most dangerous job on the PSD team. They arrive at the event at least an hour before the protectee and must remain on-site until after the protectee departs. They establish the security bubble that must be in place prior to calling the AIC and telling him it is now safe for the team and the protectee to come to the event.

Our advance teams included the two dog handlers and their explosive detection dogs, two snipers (now referred to as "designated defensive marksmen" as the term sniper has been deemed too aggressive for protection work), and usually (if we were lucky enough to be fully manned) eight other advance team members placed at various strategic locations. Once the strategic locations were identified by the advance team leader, he would set up a series of concentric security rings designed to deter and thwart—as far away from the event as possible—any attempt on the protectee's life. We wanted to make the bad guys work as hard as possible to get close to Ambassador Bremer. These rings of security included access control points where we could keep vehicles a safe distance from the event and not fear car or truck bombs exploding and collapsing the building. The access control points also ensured no one who was not authorized or permitted to be there got inside. The security rings became more and more restrictive as one got closer to the ambassador.

The advance team leader also had assigned to him a contingent of Army MPs. These men and women were armed with heavy weapons: M-240 7.62 machine guns, MH2B .50 caliber machine guns, and Mark 19 automatic 40 mm grenade launchers mounted on their armored Humvees. They provided a great visual and psychological deterrent to any bad guys who might not have been totally devoted to losing their lives in an attempted attack. These MPs were the major component of our limited Counter Assault Team (CAT) capabilities. Blackwater just did not have enough firepower or manpower to handle this task by itself. We had no automatic weapons or heavy weapons. These men and women did an outstanding job, and I have no doubt they were a major reason why we got home safely each day. They have my deepest respect and admiration.

The advance team leader placed these support assets wherever he felt they provided the best protection to ensure the safety of Ambassador Bremer. They were usually placed at the farthest access control areas, and then in strategic locations closer to where the event would take place. The advance team leader was in constant communication with these folks as he monitored the situation at each venue.

The sniper teams would be placed at the highest elevated positions available to the team so they could be used as advance spotters and warn the team if they saw trouble approaching. They also had to have the ability to take and make a kill shot out to hundreds of meters. Again, the advance team leader was in constant communication with these men. Many times these men would be placed on buildings across the street from an event or down the block from the event. They had no additional support. They worked alone on unsecured rooftops, endured the heat and the dust, and watched our backs. Truly a daunting task. These guys had balls made of brass.

The explosive-detecting dog team (dog and handler) had to walk and inspect the entire route the protectee would walk, and do a check on all vehicles parked in the vicinity of where the ambassador would be. In the heat the dogs could work about thirty minutes before they became exhausted and lost focus. The handlers had to be completely in tune with the dogs and recognize when they needed to get into an air-conditioned vehicle or inside a cool building. A mistake could be fatal.

The Iraqis were not happy about us having dogs. Dogs are considered filthy animals by many Muslims, and our dog handlers were constantly on the lookout for both hostile stray dogs that could cause grave damage to our bomb detectors and passive-aggressive Iraqis who would talk shit to the dogs instead of the handlers. I'm pretty sure the dogs didn't understand the Iraqis but they barked like hell and pulled on their leash as if to tear the throats out of the offending shit-talkers, which was hilarious to watch. It also reinforced the Iraqis' fears and increased our intimidation factor. In reality the dogs were so disciplined that they didn't do anything—including barking and gnashing teeth at the Iraqis—without a whispered command from the handler. The handlers just made it look like the dogs were out of control so people watching would think twice about getting too close. Once again, the advance team leader had to be in constant communication with these guys.

The advance team leader had a great deal of responsibility for the success of every mission—mission meaning every time we took the protectee out in public. It was not a job for the weak of heart. He had to make all the decisions and do all the coordination mentioned earlier, and had to make the decision to cancel the visit if he felt the security at the venue was not capable of keeping the protectee safe.

As AIC, I had to take all these actions into account and make sure the person I chose for this most important position could quickly evaluate and spot potential weaknesses at each and every venue. From my perspective the best candidates were guys I'd refer to as *America's Professional Terrorists*. I wanted to use, and tried to use whenever possible, guys who had served at the highest levels of U.S. military Special Operations. I wanted guys who had planned and executed raids to capture or kill people who were not anxious to see our toughest guys arrive at their homes or office. These men have examined *target folders*, mission briefs with the intelligence and information required to prepare and execute Special Ops. They have analyzed settings and setups searching for exploitable weaknesses. By actually planning and executing these offensive missions, they knew better what it would take to play defense. They knew how to make it more difficult for the bad guys to plan attacks against their protectee. My term for this is reverse engineering. How would I take this building, kill this person, kidnap that person? Then, what would make it much harder or impossible for me to do this? They reverse engineer, identify all factors that hopefully would make it impossible for bad guys to do bad things, and then put these factors into play. This was the mission for the advance team leader each and every time he went out.

After selecting the advance team leader, the next tough decision was to choose the drivers. Everybody thinks driving is easy. This is the furthest thing from the truth. A recent study done by an intelligence community think tank showed that nearly 85 percent of all attacks take place in or near vehicles. This finding dovetails with numerous other studies conducted over the last two decades by both government and private sector entities. No matter how broad or narrow the criteria used to define "an attack," the overwhelming majority occurred while the target or victim was in or around their vehicle. So it's certainly no surprise or coincidence that all the attacks that we came under during our time in Baghdad occurred during motorcade operations. Pretty sobering.

Standard operating procedure (SOP) for the bad guys is as follows: primary target is the VIP; secondary target is the limousine driver. The mind-set is: *Stop the driver, stop the motorcade.*

Keep the target in the kill zone until he is dead. The drivers cannot allow this to happen. A man can be the best shooter on the team, but those skills are only called on when we are under attack. The drivers have to show their skills every day. Each time we went out they had to be on their game. We couldn't afford for them to have a bad day. If they did, a team member might die. Or the VIP. The drivers have to be able to anticipate what's going to happen BEFORE it happens. They must see everything. Given the critical role the drivers play in keeping the principal alive, I would have preferred to have drivers who were trained to one common standard and through one training provider. In a perfect world we would have run all our drivers through one of Tony Scotti's Vehicle Dynamics Institute's (VDI) High-Risk-Environment Driving or Mission-Oriented Driving Skills (MODS) courses. VDI has a well-earned reputation for turning out some of the best drivers in the world and is the only training provider I am aware of that has the capability to objectively and scientifically evaluate a driver's capability to survive an ambush. Unfortunately, with roughly only twenty-four hours to begin protective operations with the ambassador, and with Joe Autera (VDI's lead instructor) halfway around the world, we did not have the time or the means to run a driving course or to thoroughly evaluate driving skills. Instead we asked for volunteers who had been through a high-level driving course or had previous high-level driving experiences. The volunteers were then evaluated each day.

The detail team is the last line of defense for the protectee. When all outer rings of security have been breached and the protectee is actually under fire or attack, the detail team must become the Praetorian Guards and be prepared to stand and fight and die. Coming from a Marine Corps background, I wanted guys who had some type of military infantry experience. Marine grunts, Army Rangers, guys from the 82nd Airborne Division, or street cops from tough cities who very often had to rely on their instincts to survive—these are the guys accustomed to following orders without question and without blinking, guys who would stand and fight and give their lives if necessary. I needed men who could see problems happening and respond appropriately— and not necessarily with violence. The detail team members were always close to the protectee and thus were often in the newspapers or on TV. They became famous back home because people saw them standing next to the man. They were the rock stars of the PSD team.

The shift leader of the detail team had the responsibility for all tactical decisions during a mission. He was my eyes and ears. He watched the formations and gave direction to the team while my sole focus as AIC was the protectee. I rode in the front-right seat of the "limo" and basically remained mute while a mission was under way. I monitored all the radio traffic and chimed in if I felt it was necessary, but usually I did not want Ambassador Bremer to hear us talking about potential dangers. Our job was to allow him to do his job without even thinking about what we are doing.

As AIC I was ultimately responsible for all aspects of the pro- tection operation and made all the final decisions. I was also the only one to ever communicate directly with the protectee. My job on a mission was to be no farther than one arm's length from the

VIP, and to be ready to use my body as a shield between him and any potential attackers. As AIC I liaised with the ambassador's staff and made sure that all coordination was done between the various groups involved. I kept on top of the schedule at all times and directly received intel reports from all sources. A failure in any aspect of the PSD team's operation rested, ultimately, on my shoulders. I knew, if our team was good, I would get the credit. Likewise, if something went wrong, I would be accountable.

One of the toughest parts of being the AIC was honestly evaluating team members. I had to make sure that round pegs were plugged into round holes, and square pegs into square holes. No one can be expected to do a job he is incapable of doing. A leader's most important task is to make sure he never puts a person in a position to fail. Different backgrounds and personalities mean each person has specific strengths and weaknesses, and thus each is capable or incapable of performing certain duties. In a combat zone each job has responsibilities that must *always* be performed correctly. A mistake could be fatal. Placing the right people in these jobs was initially a huge headache as nobody knew exactly what we were going to need to do. Friendship, family, prior relationships, etc., could not influence the decision-making process. Either someone could do the job or he couldn't. Needless to say I managed to hurt the feelings of more than a few guys when I made the decision that they were not good enough for certain positions. In the end the guys I thought were best suited for each position were placed in those positions.

For the ambassador's Red Zone missions we ran a three-car motorcade consisting of a lead car, the limo, and a follow car.

The lead car had the tactical commander (TC) in the right-front seat, a driver, and two shooters (detail members) sitting in the rear seats. In the rear of the vehicle we had an additional man referred to as the well-agent. Whenever possible I wanted the well-agent to be a medic.

While the motorcade was moving the TC was responsible for communicating with all our support assets (helicopters, MP CAT teams, etc.). He monitored oncoming and merging traffic, and relayed this info to the shift leader. All his senses were tuned to search for potential threats and ambushes. He called out threats, and if traffic was bad, he ordered the switch to one of the alternate, preplanned routes. The team adjusted its movements to his premonitions.

The protectee and any VIPs accompanying him rode in the limo with the driver and me (AIC). The follow car had the shift leader sitting in the right-front seat, a driver, two shooters in the rear seats, and usually another medic (well-agent) in the third seat. It was important to have this second medic in the follow car. If the limo was attacked, plans called for the lead car to engage the enemy while we transferred the ambassador to the follow car. If he was injured, we had to be able to treat his wounds as quickly as possible.

We also had another contingent of Army MPs assigned to act as our CAT team element during any movements that we made with the ambassador. Again, my hat is off to these folks.

Attached to our team were two guys (later trimmed down to one) who would handle all the operations support and logistics management taking place in the background for all team members. They coordinated the ID cards, found bed space, checked on trailer accommodations, issued and tracked guns and gear, wrangled with the all-too-regular updates to the ambassador's schedule, and kept me in the loop on any and all changes. As it turns out, with the contract business's reverse pyramid model of tooth-to-tail support, these guys ended up as seat-of-the-pants jacks-of-all-trades. They found themselves doing all the behind-the-scenes support functions a military organization typically has large groups of people around to handle: supply, administration, travel, payroll, logistics, weapons repair, communications watch. They were savvy and resourceful and could buy, beg, borrow, or trade for the necessities to support a thirty-six-man team in a war zone—any and all the things the team couldn't do for themselves while they were on the road keeping the ambassador safe. They scrounged office space, computers, telephone and computer hookups, office furniture, computers, beds, bullets, batteries, maps, and even got the chow hall to make sure the team was fed after the kitchen closed during late nights. They had their hands full and literally made it up on their own as they went, as I was always with the ambassador or attending a meeting someplace else.

After the Secret Service named Ambassador Bremer the most-threatened man in the world I began to get daily intelligence briefs from the various intelligence agencies—CIA, DIA, OSS, and State Department—working in the country. The agencies all had the same intelligence information, but each, depending upon the analyst and his source, interpreted it slightly differently and relayed it to me with a personal twist. Still, they all had the same basic message—"Uh, not sure how to tell you this, but today, you are all going to die."

It was enlightening and frightening at the same time. I was never sure how much info to share with guys on the team. I was worried that some guys I did not know well might overreact to something and create an incident. My intuition eventually proved prophetic as other Blackwater teams did things that came under intense scrutiny in the years after we left. Why some of these incidents occurred, I will never know. But I do know, on my team, especially in the beginning, there were some guys looking for an excuse to try to prove their manhood. Many times we were in a position that could have resulted in us shooting people, and being completely justified in doing so. Calm heads were mandatory.

All this hit the guys within twenty-four hours of the team getting "boots on the ground." Throw in trying to figure out which radios we would use, who would work where, getting ID cards, fighting with the CID about which vehicles we would use, and an average person would be inclined to get a tad short-tempered. The stress was immense. It felt like I was being kicked every time I turned around. There was always an excuse as to why I could not get what I needed. Simple requests became like acts of Congress in their complexity. And all we were trying to do was keep the ambassador alive.

Four days after the Secret Service left—and after twenty-four hours of intense construction modifications—the villa they had selected for the ambassador was ready for his occupancy. I chose a team of guys to safeguard this house 24/7. It had been the home of the mother-in-law of Uday Hussein, one of Saddam's sons. It was garish but had extremely thick walls we hoped could withstand an explosion. In the rear of the place were two other buildings we could use to store some of our gear. Ominously, one of them had hooks in the ceilings from which, we were told, the Hussein brothers used to hang their enemies. We even found several handguns that had been left in various locations around the property—in the outbuildings, on the roof, in the garden. It was pretty bizarre.

Guarding Bremer's sleeping quarters was not part of the initial Blackwater contract, but we had to make it work. Six of my new thirty-four men were designated to go and secure the villa. It was not quite the glamorous "world-famous bodyguard" job for which they'd signed up. Everybody wanted to be on the team with the boss. Feelings were hurt, and in the beginning some guys thought being assigned to the villa meant they were on the B-team and somehow unworthy. No job on the detail was any less important than any other job. Everybody had to pull their weight and do the assigned task to the best of their ability. I put one of my men, Sax, at the villa initially to oversee the security enhancements and to make sure that the guys were doing the job as we had outlined. Sax was a former SEAL, and he took over the villa and ran it well. All this was accomplished in short order, and I moved him over to the advance team.

So, doing the math, out of thirty-four men I had two Ops/support guys, six guys at the villa, and two dog handlers, leaving just twenty-six people (this included Bird and me) for the advance team and the detail. The advance team always went out with the two dog guys and twelve men. That left eleven for the detail; with room for one man being sick, hurt, or otherwise incapacitated.

The food was well below American standards, the heat was unbearable, jet lag exacerbated problems, and still the team hit the ground running roughly one day after landing. Coordinating everything each day became a logistical nightmare. Guys were sick, tired, cranky, and some just plain should not have been there. In the haste to put the team together, the selection process was not as stringent as it would eventually become. We found out very quickly who the "real men" were and who the pretenders were. Guys complained about the hours and said they were being overworked and forced to miss meals. Some complained I was working them too hard and they were not getting enough sleep. Some complained about the living conditions, some about the food. My response was pretty much always the same, "If the ambassador can do it, so can we. If you want to go home, just ask."

The typical day began at 0530 with the detail meeting in front of the palace before heading over to the ambassador's villa. We would get to the villa, talk to the guys there, and see how the night had gone; then we'd form up security around the building to ensure that if an attack happened we could get the ambassador back into the house or into the armored vehicle as quickly as possible. He left the villa around 0630 each morning to begin his day. This happened every single day we were there. The route to the palace was a short motorcade trip, but nevertheless strict mental discipline needed to be maintained. We could never let our guard down. We would arrive at the office, form the security formation around the motorcade, and escort the ambassador into the palace. Once inside his office we posted one man to stay at the door and another outside the office to man the metal detectors and work with our MP escort team to keep unauthorized people from entering. The MPs were invaluable in this position as they had the power to arrest anyone who defied their orders to stop. Many people (military and nonmilitary) were in the habit of carrying weapons with them everywhere they went. We did NOT and would not allow any weapons, except for the ones that the Blackwater guys were carrying, inside the ambassador's office. It became an issue more than a few times. Without the MPs' presence, I'm sure it would have gotten very ugly.

There was a one-hour rotation of the posts around the office, thirty minutes on his door and thirty minutes at the metal detectors. We tried to make sure no one ever had more than one office shift each day so everyone was as fresh as possible. When the ambassador went to the chow hall, we would send a few guys down ahead of time to get him a table and try to give him some space. Ambassador Bremer, however, would shake hands with everyone and pose for pictures with whoever asked (including the non-Americans). With daily intel reports indicating the kitchen staff, the barbers, the groundskeepers, and many others were potential assassins, my guys were in a constant state of high alert. And this was INSIDE the Green Zone.

The ambassador also kept an extremely heavy schedule of meetings outside the Green Zone. Each mission required the advance team to head out an hour or so before the detail team to run the routes and establish security around the venue. Then the detail team would take the ambassador to the event. Then we would head back to the palace and resume security at the office while we waited for the next mission. This happened anywhere from once to five or six times a day, each and every day for the entire time we provided his protection.

Around 1900 each day, I would ask Bremer what time he wanted to go back to the villa. The answer varied from 2100 to 2300 And this was only if a member of the governance team had not barged in on him at the last second to talk about the latest crisis du jour. The governance team was composed of the Americans and Iraqis who were trying to design and implement a new Iraqi government. They had a very difficult job. Every day there was a new problem; every evening the ambassador was updated on wrinkles in yesterday's plan. Oftentimes he would ask for a 2100 departure only to be trapped in his office until midnight. The detail team staged thirty minutes before his requested departure time. Sometimes it was three hours or more before he actually loaded up in the car and we took him home. The boss was a machine. Upon arrival at the villa he would usually tell me to be there at 0630 again the next day. The detail would then head back to their trailers after securing their gear and weapons. Five and a half hours later we were back to work.

About a week after landing, the team was able to move into their trailers from the makeshift barracks created from the small ballroom Saddam had in the palace. Of course this was only accomplished because Colonel Dennis Sabol (USMC—assigned to Ambassador Bremer's staff) put priority on the Blackwater guys getting housing before a few "less essential" people who were working there. Colonel Sabol was a good man who more than once helped me navigate through some potentially murky situations. You have to love the Marine Corps brotherhood.

The guys moved into a trailer park, and essentially had an entire block to themselves. This quickly became known as Black-water Boulevard. Our mission had morphed from what we had anticipated. We had been promised armored vehicles and had none; we had not been told about the villa detail; we did not know Ambassador Bremer never rested and never took more than four hours off. The big boy rules I had inherited from Bird became the norm. I was not going to tell the guys they could not enjoy a cold beer at the end of an eighteen-hour day. My only rule was if you showed up drunk or could not function at 100 percent the next day, you would be sent home.

Being true type A personalities, the end of the day get-togeth-ers began to draw quite a crowd. When a group of alpha males congregate there is no limit on where the conversation may head. And we were quite a diverse collection of former Rangers, SEALs, Recon Marines, Special Forces, French Foreign Legion, SWAT cops, regular navy, regular army, and cops. The ball bust-ing could reach the hysterical stage in seconds. Nothing was off-limits—interservice rivalries, country boy vs. city boy, North vs. South, football vs. baseball, Army vs. Navy vs. Marines vs. Air Force. And being, by and large, a group of intelligent, self-con-fident, quick-witted, experienced, and extremely sarcastic guys, there was neither room nor time for guys who did not have truly thick skin. It was a comedy show that people outside our group often found irresistible. Of course, the outsiders also became targets of opportunity, and many gave as well as they took.

No one at the palace really knew what to make of us. They knew why we were there, but Blackwater at this time meant little or nothing to most people. We were the quiet professionals struggling to find our place in the grand scheme of palace politics and palace life. We were trying to keep the ambassador alive while he kept a schedule we were convinced was designed to kill us. We were there when most people arrived for work in the morning, and we were still there long after they left for the evening. If they showed up for the midnight meal we were still there. Despite gruff, intimidating appearances most of the guys were charming and polite to everyone who approached, and they were always ready with a smile and a self-deprecating sense of humor. It did not take long to become well liked and a true part of the Coalition Provisional Authority (CPA) community. The guys were soon embraced not as knuckle-dragging Neanderthal morons but as serious professionals doing a serious job and having a good time while they were doing it.

We began to get invited to the pool parties that were held every Thursday evening. We rarely got there when they started, but the guys would eventually show up and friendships were formed with many from the different groups—U.S. and foreign military types, U.S. and foreign politicians, career government workers, and some remarkable civilians who had volunteered to be part of this massive undertaking—the rebuilding of Iraq.

Coordinating with other groups that were to attend a function with Ambassador Bremer was one of the toughest parts of my job. It involved talking to other security teams, the press, military leaders, and anyone else who was attending. As the team protecting the highest-ranking man in the country, we always had final say on all security arrangements that would affect our ability to make the event as safe as possible for the ambassador. There was always a good bit of give-and-take on all sides. As a result people began to trust us. They realized we were only looking out for the ambassador and not trying (intentionally) to make anyone's job more difficult. We recognized as well that they had a job to do. By working together we could all do our jobs better.

And many of the people we had to liaise with were attractive females.

The ratio of men to women was roughly forty to one. Each woman there probably had in the vicinity of a hundred or so guys trying to woo her heart. My guys were no exception. But they were experienced hunters who knew how to charm. With their past lives as special operations ass kickers and the aura they currently had as Blackwater PSD team members, they did not lack the confidence to try to claim a sizable share of the attention of the limited supply of the fair gender.

Realizing quickly that this could pose some problems, we had to establish ground rules to keep guys from fighting over the same lady. The rules were pretty easy to understand and eventually became ingrained in how we dealt with relationships. All women were considered fair game until a member of the team slept with her. After that she was off-limits to all other Blackwater guys. A gentleman's agreement if you will. And it worked. There were very few fights or arguments over women. We all knew and obeyed the rules. The woman chose the guy she wanted; we respected her decision, and the other wolves left her alone.

About a week or so after we took over the PSD duties, the ambassador was called back to Washington. This gave us a chance to finally test fire and zero our weapons, work on our formations and evac drills, and to unwind and get to know one another. Bird and I decided to throw a party. We really knew nothing about the guys on the team, and I did not want anything stupid to happen this early in the game, so we had it at the Al Rasheed pool not at the palace. We grabbed six guys, grabbed our weapons, put on our body armor, and headed to downtown Baghdad to buy some adult beverages. In downtown Baghdad there were a few stores that sold liquor, and somehow Bird knew where they were and what types of beverages were available at each. It was always the same routine. Drive up, jump out, establish a security perimeter around the vehicles, dash in, quickly order what we wanted, and dash back to the vehicles. Total time on station was usually less than five minutes. Then we'd race back to the Green Zone. Of course, we always made sure that if anyone outside our team wanted something we would also get it for them. Eventually we became the go-to guys for many Green Zone workers who had no access to vehicles or a way to get outside. We were a full-service, happy, and friendly bunch.

We returned and talked the guys at the chow hall into giving us some ice, which was always in extremely short supply. Then we headed over to the Al Rasheed. As luck would have it quite a few people accepted our invitation. All told there were probably twenty-five of our guys, an additional twenty from other groups, and a handful of women. As the party reached its zenith everyone eventually wound up in the pool. The shirts came off, then the shorts. The ladies present got a lot of attention.

Type A personalities in a war zone are driven by many things. One is survival. I knew these guys would fight to the death if they needed to. They were tough, in top shape, and had great skill sets honed over the course of impressive careers. The other overwhelming drive they had was driven by testosterone. They were men, and men like women. Some guys were married, some divorced, most had kids, but all wanted female companionship. They were very intelligent and had the "A" game that emboldened them to say and do most anything in the pursuit of a woman. Interestingly, many times they were not the hunters but the prey. The war zone equally drew type A ladies.

Nudity in our world is not a big deal. Special operations guys have few or no hang-ups about their bodies. Guys get naked at the drop of a hat. Sometimes in somewhat awkward situations—because they think it might be funny, or they just feel like it, or someone dares them—next thing you know there's a naked dude sitting right next to you. We just laugh because it's a pretty normal thing for us. For others, it can be a real turnoff. Fortunately, the women who joined us for our get-togethers had no issues with it. The next thing I knew they were down to bras and thongs.

The party shaped up nicely, but I was very apprehensive about it getting out of hand. As the sun went down I suggested we retreat to Blackwater Boulevard. We loaded up the remaining beer and liquor and as many of the guys we could find, and back to the palace grounds we went.

Because Bird and I had moved in before there was even a thought of Blackwater taking over the PSD duties, our trailer was directly behind the palace and about five hundred yards from the Boulevard. I cruised over to my trailer, put on some dry clothes, and headed back to the guys. When I arrived, the party had grown from just us to more than seventy-five people. The music was blasting and the laughter was even louder. Everyone was getting along fine. Bonding with the team and relaxing had been a good idea. Everyone got to know each other a little better, and I was hopeful that this was harbinger of good things to come.

In most groups there is a 10 percent factor that does not belong or cannot get along with the other 90 percent. This will always remain a mystery to me. The day after the party the bullshit started. We had a guy assigned to the team who had apparently not done well during the selection process but was sent over anyway because he could speak Arabic. I was told he was to be used strictly as an interpreter, and I assigned him to Scotty H, who was in charge of the advance team. Scotty was a retired, no-nonsense SEAL I truly respected. He is one of the best men I have worked with anywhere in the world. He ran a tight ship and did an excellent job despite the short run-up to going operational.

We had certain rules that everyone had to follow. We all had to wear collared shirts whenever we were out on a mission. No thigh holsters, no ball caps, no full beards. I wanted us to present a professional appearance in keeping with Ambassador Bremer's status as the presidential envoy. There were a lot of other PSD teams running around looking like an advertisement for *Soldier of Fortune* magazine. That was not going to be us. There was even a guy who walked around the palace wearing a three-quarter-length leather duster with a sword strapped to his back. He was not with us or part of us.

The interpreter—my first problem child of many to follow—approached me one afternoon after he had an argument with Ski (a former SEAL now running the operational side for me) and stated that he had "more combat experience than anyone else" on the team and wanted to be a shooter assigned to the detail. I laughed and told him it would never happen. He said he was going to call Blackwater and complain. I told him to be my guest, and offered him my phone. I then told him if he could not get with the program he would soon have one of two choices—an aisle or window seat back to the United States. He stormed off muttering.

The very next mission we ran this guy showed up in a black T-shirt and with a ball cap on his head. As luck would have it the ambassador spotted him immediately and gruffly asked me if he was one of mine. FUCK ME! I got Scotty on the radio and told him to have the guy disappear, and that we'd deal with it when we got back to the palace. We got back and I told Ken H (my chief Ops/support guy) to start the process to get rid of him.

Firing a man in the war zone presented some unique obstacles. One: There were no commercial flights, so getting someone out of the country took about three days to arrange while we coordinated with the Air Force to find a seat available for the screwup. And believe me, the Air Force was busy as hell transporting people who were far more important to the war effort, as well as wounded people and soldiers. Dealing with a Blackwater headache was not high priority. Two: These guys had access to weapons, and we were never sure how one would react to being fired.

Ken looked at me and we both laughed as we really had no idea on how to make this happen. But Ken was an extremely smart guy. He never took no for an answer, and always killed everybody with kindness. And he always got what we needed when we needed it. To this day, I will never know how he accomplished all that he did. He was a trusted ally and an invaluable member of the team.

Ken went to work on the issue, and said he had secured a seat on an Air Force C-130 for the guy to Amman in three days. I called Blackwater and told them they needed to get this guy a plane ticket to his home of record from Amman and they said they would. The program manager back in Moyock was not happy with me over his firing. This would be the beginning of many attempts by this guy sitting back stateside to question my decisions, or to interfere with running the detail, even though he had no idea what was the in-country ground truth.

Now I had to figure out what to do with this renegade for three days. I did not want a disgruntled employee wandering around with weapons, and I certainly did not want him embarrassing me again. The decision was made to let him continue working until the departure date. I held my breath and my tongue each day. I was embarrassed and disgusted at the same time.

On the day he left I sent three guys over to his trailer at 0600 to collect his weapons, and to tell him he had one hour to pack before we took him directly to the airport. He complied meekly and off he went. This was the way I ended up firing any of the guys who got sent home. They had no time to stew or get angry, and by the time the shock wore off they were on a plane home. It worked for me—and for the team.

About this time I got a call from Blackwater asking if I would extend for another thirty days. The pay would go up to $675 a day, and as I had not yet been killed I figured, *What the hell!* I called Kim and told her, and she agreed that another thirty days was not such a big deal. Of course, by this time I had been on TV, in the newspapers, and in magazines in pictures with the ambassador and did not realize the toll it was taking on the family. Katherine had it the hardest as she was in high school and had to deal with the antiwar liberals who saw me every morning on the news channels. But she stood up to them and told them that both her dad and her uncle John (US Army, Special Forces—Afghanistan) were away fighting for the country. I was, and am, very proud of her.

I talked to Bird. "Blackwater called and asked me to extend. They want you to extend also."

"Yeah," he said. "Good luck with that. I took another gig for 1K a day [$1,000 per day]!"

"Damn! Any way I can talk you out of it?"

"Zero chances of that happening. Good luck. You know you're going to get killed, don't you?"

"I hope the fuck not."

"Look at some of these guys they sent over. I can get you on the same gig with me."

"Thanks, but I told them I'd stay."

"You've lost your damn mind."

"Only time will tell."

He had accepted a gig with another company doing security work in the sandbox. To say I was bummed would be a gross understatement. I was losing a good friend and my shift leader at the same time. And now I had to find someone who was as good as he was. That person was not there at this time. It was a scary proposition.

Bird left five days later. With the loss of the guy I fired and Bird, my thirty-six-man team was now a thirty-four-man team.

The operational tempo continued at breakneck speed. We had four or five missions every day. Up at 0530, done around midnight. We were running the roads in Baghdad as safely as we could but traffic was a bitch, and the intel reports came in every day about our pending demise. We would jump the median and drive against oncoming traffic before we would ever allow ourselves to be stopped for more than a few seconds. The MP CAT team would speed ahead of us and block intersections so we rarely if ever stopped. Arrivals and departures were rehearsed until we could get in and out of the open area as quickly as possible. The guys were finally all in tune with one another and had learned to fill and flow. If a guy was out of position, someone would automatically move to the vacated spot. I was pleased.

Lydia K, a member of the Governance Team, was working closely with the local Iraqis and the ambassador. She came to me one day and told me that the local population was becoming

angry about the way our guys were pointing weapons at everyone on the street as the motorcade moved through town. The
lead and follow cars were not armored vehicles and the new shift
leader thought it was a good idea to have the guys hold their
weapons through the open windows so "they could react more
quickly." Quite honestly I had never thought of the reaction
of the locals, but Lydia was very in touch with the locals and I
trusted her. If she said something might become a problem, I
knew she was right and it would eventually become a problem.
I went to the new shift leader and told him that from now on
all weapons would be kept inside the vehicles and the windows
would be rolled up. To say he was not happy would be an understatement. I pointed out that Bird had always kept the weapons
below the closed windows. He still wanted to argue about it. Oh
well, I said, it is my call and if you do not agree do you want a
window seat or an aisle seat? The weapons stayed in the cars with
the windows up from that point forward.

I was still short two guys. Shrek, a former FAST Company
(Fleet Anti-Terrorism Security) Marine, showed up and filled
one of the holes. It was apparent that he had some experience,
and he went to work almost immediately. We still had guys with
gastrointestinal issues or upper respiratory infections from the
never-ending dust. And the heat was a killer. And now another 10
percenter revealed himself. A former cop asked to speak to me.
He told me that he had not signed up for this type of work, that
he was used to eight-hour days, three meals per day, coffee breaks,
and eight hours of sleep. I very sarcastically told him to organize
a union and see what he could get arranged. I was faced now with

sending another guy home, but in a stroke of clarity I decided to send him to the villa and replace him with a villa guy. The villa guy was ecstatic to be on the detail, and the weak sister could relax as he would no longer have to go into the Red Zone. The villa quickly became a place where I could hide the sick, lame, and lazy.

Baghdad was a city that was one of the most extreme examples that I have ever seen of "haves" and "have-nots." Saddam's palaces were a garish testament to excess. Huge chandeliers, gold-plated fixtures in the bathrooms, fifty-foot cathedral ceilings, pictures of Hussein in every room. He spared no expense in making sure he had the best of everything. The citizens of Baghdad, on the other hand, lived in cement houses that had no sewage systems and no organized garbage pickup. Raw sewage ran from the houses into the streets; garbage was tossed in vacant lots. The smell, intensified by the heat, was oppressive. Electricity was a hit-or-miss proposition for the people. Forget about air-conditioning. Saddam had kept his foot firmly on the throats of his people while he enjoyed all the luxuries that he or anyone else could ever imagine. No wonder they hated him.

OCTOBER 2003—THE LITTLE BIRDS ARRIVE

About this time I got a call from Blackwater that my helicopters would be arriving in a few days. Once again I was faced with a logistical nightmare. I now needed housing for ten more people, and a place to park and be able to work on the "Little Birds." I went to Ken H and asked him to get the process rolling. There was a helo landing zone (LZ Washington) in the Green Zone that would be perfect, but there was neither housing nor a hangar there. Ken went to Colonel Sabol and somehow between the two of them, they miraculously got trailers installed at the LZ, and construction on a hangar began.

Six pilots, four mechanics, and the three MD-530 helicopters arrived. I met with the lead pilot. We talked about potential problems that might arise, and he assured me that due to his connections with the army air guys he could handle the issues. All the pilots in the first group were former TF-160 guys—The Night Stalkers. Most had considerable time working with Delta and the SEALs in support of spec-ops missions. Several were veteran pilots of the famous Somalia incident immortalized in the film *Black Hawk Down*. Most had retired from active duty after twenty years.

It took a couple of days for the Little Birds to be assembled, op checked, and declared operational. The decision was made to use only two at any time, thus making sure we would always have a spare ready to go if one of them got hit or had a mechanical issue. Each bird had two pilots and room in the back for two shooters who might provide firepower and cover in the event the motorcade was hit.

And then, as I anticipated and feared, some issues began to develop. Apparently a couple of the pilots never got the memo they were there to support the PSD team that was providing the security to the most-threatened man in the world. Several seemed to think our PSD team was there to support the new air wing of Blackwater. This was the first time that Blackwater had an aviation division, and, by extension, the first time that air power would be used to provide support to a PSD team on the ground. Just like when building the PSD team, we would have to develop the protocols for this new air resource. First these pilots wanted me to give them dedicated door gunners who would report only to them. When I told them I didn't have sufficient manpower to do that, they suggested I cut back on either the detail or the advance team. Really? How would that make sense? Where did they think we were working, Myrtle Beach? I told them when the guys from the villa were off duty, they could use them. It was the best I could do until we got more people.

Then they informed me that, per FAA regulations, they could only be on duty for eight hours each day. WTF? We were in Iraq, not Nebraska! Again, I told them we worked whenever the ambassador worked. They wanted precise takeoff times and wanted to know exactly when they should be back on station before the ambassador left a meeting. I'll never know what fairy tales they had been told, but they had obviously not been given a clear picture of what we were really doing. Meetings lasted until the ambassador was done. Sometimes they ended twenty minutes early; sometimes they ran two hours over. Ambassador Bremer was trying to rebuild a country, and a few of the pilots were worried about crew rest? I was beside myself. One pilot actually told me to tell the ambassador that he had to follow his schedule exactly or it would affect the pilots' performance. It was an amazing conversation. He's looking at me like I'm crazy, and

I'm looking at him like he has three heads. I looked around for a *Candid Camera* crew. There was no way he could be serious. But he was.

At this point I wasn't even sure how to best utilize them in their support role. A few days later one of the pilots came over to talk to me. Steve "Hacksaw" Chilton knew I was reaching a breaking point, and he asked me to let him massage his boss. I knew from word of mouth Hacksaw was a straight shooter and a damn good pilot, and I knew if he told me something could be done and that he could do it, it would get done. He was also, far and away, the best pilot in the group.

Somehow he fixed the issues. How he did it will always remain a mystery. I did hear a few stories of rather heated arguments and offers to "step outside" to handle the differences of opinion. Fortunately they kept that strictly to themselves.

The first Thursday the pilots were in-country I invited them over to my trailer for some adult beverages; I was told curtly by the lead pilot that his guys would not be attending. I responded in kind. I said they now worked for me; I was the AIC, and he and his guys fell under my command, not vice versa. He did not come over, but a few of the others did. It was the start of a very contentious relationship between him and me. I was never happier than when he rotated out. Eventually I learned that his biggest issue stemmed from taking directions from me, a former Marine Corps NCO, an enlisted man. He was a retired army colonel, and he truly believed that officers were superior to enlisted men in everything and in every way. The fact that I had been doing protection operations for years for a former cabinet-level government official meant nothing to him. As an officer he automatically knew more about protection than I ever would.

The other pilots were great guys—absolutely fearless. Men of character who would do anything asked of them whenever it was asked. And ask we did, and answer the call they did.

At this time Blackwater had another team in country—The Dirty 30. They worked under a different contract and provided support for a different agency. Most were former spec-op guys (Recon, SEALs, and Special Forces) and when they heard about our Little Birds they could not get to me fast enough to see how they might use them to support their mission. Once again, I had to remind people that the birds were here to support the PSD team guarding Ambassador Bremer. I got the patented Blackwater "one team, one fight" speech, and I realized that they actually thought they had access to the helos. It was a nightmare. We were on different contracts, being paid by different government agencies. If something happened while we were out with the ambassador, how was I supposed to explain why my birds were providing air support for someone else?

My new toys were a novelty item to most of the folks in the palace. Everyone wanted a ride or to "borrow" them. It was a pain in the ass dealing with all the requests for special favors from folks who "absolutely needed" them for some special project. I tried to stay focused on the missions, but between the attitude of the lead pilot and the hours my men were keeping, it was a brutal struggle. The lead pilot never met a request he thought he shouldn't fulfill. In his mind those "recreational" flights would count against his eight-hour day and had the potential to generate future business and income for Blackwater Air. Needless to say they were rarely granted. The guy was a skilled pilot, but why he was there as the lead guy baffled me. We made up the rules as the situations dictated, and he played everything by the book—a book that was totally inapplicable in Iraq. He would call Blackwater HQ daily to complain about something, and then my phone would ring and I would be asked to explain some nonexistent problem. On more than one occasion I was with the ambassador when Blackwater called about some slight, real or imagined, that hurt this guy's feelings. I only called HQ if and when I had an emergency.

At this time IEDs (improvised explosive devices) were becoming quite a problem for the folks (military and civilian) in Baghdad. The Iraqis were masters of taking different explosives—artillery shells, mortar shells, hand grenades, plastic explosives, etc.—and turning them into explosive devices they could bury under the road, stuff into animal carcasses, or hide in trash cans and then detonate remotely. IEDs were extremely effective and were responsible for thousands of American, coalition, and Iraqi citizens' injuries and deaths. Not to mention the car bombs that were driven by suicide bombers or the suicide bombers that would strap explosives to themselves and walk up to the target and blow themselves up while killing their intended victims.

Consequently, we were always on guard for lone individuals. One day, we took Bremer to the other side of The 14th of July Bridge. This bridge crossed the Euphrates River and was named by the Iraqis to honor a special date in their history. A homeless man approached the motorcade while we were stopped for traffic. He fixated on the limo and began to approach with a broom in one hand. The other hand extended palm up. He was obviously begging for a handout. The limo driver, instead of keeping the car moving, reached and fumbled for his pistol as though he was going to draw it and fire it through the armored window. I casually reached over and stopped him from drawing the weapon. Firing a weapon inside an armored vehicle may be just about dumbest thing a person could do. The bullet can't get out. It would just bounce around inside until it hit one of us or the ambassador. At the same time I heard yelling behind me and turned around to see the shift leader out of his vehicle pointing his weapon at the homeless guy and screaming at him to stop and get back. Funny thing about the English language; no matter how loud you yell it, if they can't understand it, they can't understand it. The ambassador calmly asked me if it was necessary to point a loaded weapon at an obviously homeless beggar. I told him I would talk to the team. Fuck.

In October the Al Rasheed Hotel came under a rocket attack that killed an army Special Forces soldier and badly wounded several others. The rocket launcher used in the attack was a large, hollowed-out diesel generator with drop sides that had been towed into place by a pickup truck. The truck had pulled up, stopped, and the driver had gotten out to initiate the launch. The generator held a bunch of rockets in improvised launch tubes set to fire when a countdown timer hit zero. The timer clicked, the sides dropped, and some rockets launched. Lucky for most of the folks in the hotel, only about eight of the array (I don't recall the exact total number, around twenty to twenty-five, I think) went off. That was the trouble with the improvised munitions that the Iraqis started slapping together. Sometimes they worked, sometimes they didn't. Who knows how many attacks didn't happen because of shoddy and poor quality of work.

Thank God this had not happened the evening of our first party a few weeks earlier. Prior to this the Al Rasheed had been viewed as a safe place for us to go. Another fantasy destroyed.

As a result of the attack, the decision was made to close the hotel to all Americans, and to move all U.S. personnel onto the palace grounds. This created another housing shortage as the trailer parks were still under construction. Steve Jones and Bill Miller approached me and asked if we had any beds available that they could use. Both were Diplomatic Security (DS) agents for the U.S. State Department. I liked both of them—great guys on assignment to help transition the palace grounds to the new U.S. embassy in Baghdad. Bill would actually become the first regional security officer (RSO) in the new Iraq.

Thanks to Ken H's efforts liaising with a navy officer, LCDR Tucker, (whom he had met and formed a great working relationship with in the palace), we had secured a large multiroom office and a separate cipher-locked room with cots that we used as a "ready" room where the guys could relax between missions. There was a refrigerator and long-distance phone line for the team to call family back home. Inside the locked room we stored our weapons and operational gear. It wasn't much, but it beat the hell out of living in tents. Bill and Steve and another DS agent moved in that day and lived there for a few weeks. Bill, even before becoming the RSO, had become a valuable ally to Blackwater. He helped me get a lot of things accomplished through both back channels and official channels that otherwise may have never gotten done.

In late 2003 Bill stopped an international incident that would have been a disaster. Secretary of State Colin Powell came to town for a visit, and made several trips with Ambassador Bremer during the days he was there. One of the visits was to the Baghdad City Council in downtown Baghdad, a Red Zone destination we truly hated each and every time we went there. The DS team accompanying the secretary worked very closely with both our detail team and our advance team. The AIC for the secretary was John Murphy. John is and was a great guy, and he's still a good friend. Post-Iraq I worked with John for about seven years in the Anti-Terrorism Assistance Program run by the U.S. State Department.

Knowing that eventually the palace grounds would become the U.S. embassy, and speculating that if Blackwater was still doing security there, a decent working relationship with the State Department would be important, I offered John any support we could provide. On this particular day my advance team had gone to the Baghdad City Council and had begun setting up the concentric rings of security that we needed to protect both the ambassador and the secretary. One of the DS advance agents panicked when he saw Iraqis in the street carrying AK-47s. To us it meant almost nothing; every family in Iraq had at least one AK-47. It only became an issue when and if they pointed them at us . . . which they frequently did. They were extremely careless about their weapons handling. The DS agent ordered my snipers to shoot each and every Iraqi carrying a rifle. Fortunately, Scotty, my advance team leader, called me and told me what was happening. I told the guys they were not to shoot at anybody unless they were fired upon first. I then called Bill Miller, and he called the agent and told him to follow Blackwater's lead when it came to this sort of thing. Nisoor Square would have been nothing compared to this disaster had Bill not intervened and ordered his agents to comply with our tactics and protocols.

The intel reports continued to get darker and darker. The Iraqis were becoming more openly hostile to all American forces, and the threats against Bremer continued to pour in. One day I got a report that the insurgents had decided that Bremer did not have enough security guys close to him and he would be susceptible to a knife or suicide bomber attack. At this time I was still wearing a sport coat and trying to blend in. I made the decision to begin dressing like the rest of the Blackwater guys with weapons revealed, making no attempt to hide who or why I was there and letting folks know that we were right in the ambassador's back pocket. Two days later another report was passed along stating that the insurgents had decided to attack the British ambassador instead because Bremer now had security close to him and the British ambassador did not. Needless to say my British counterparts were not happy with me.

Being proper British military they continued to dress as protocol dictated. It sucked to be them. We laughed like hell. They were some of the best guys and gals I had ever met—men and women who were extremely professional, hard, and very funny—top-shelf operators and world-class ballbusters. In the austere environment of high-threat protection, emotions run high. These emotions can eat you alive if you let them. Only professionals with a great sense of humor tend to thrive. Anyone who has ever worked or visited the United Kingdom can appreciate the British sense of humor. For those who have not, let's just say it is not quite the same as American humor.

Our British counterparts, the security detail protecting Ambassador Greenstock, was composed of active-duty military from the British army. They were a lively bunch of real professionals, and my men quickly grew to become good friends with them. We spent a lot of time together, and I'm still in contact with many of them. True to their word, the Brits had offered any and all support we might require. Being British military, they had far more assets than we did.

For example, after the first IED attack on the palace area in early November 2003, one of our guys we called Geek (former Air Force Special Operations) was able to secure a Mini Me, or what we know as the M249 squad automatic weapon, from the Brits, which he carried on the advance team. The Brits let him borrow it for his entire stay in Iraq. To be honest I never asked him about it because I didn't want to know how exactly he obtained that weapon system. He got it, I was glad. It was better for me not to know.

Among their various forms of entertainment the Brits played "the whaah game." It went something like this. You ask someone a blatantly obvious question, such as "Are those blue jeans you are wearing?" The person replies with a look that questions your intelligence and says something to the effect of, "Yes, I am." The person playing the game yells as loud and as annoyingly as possible: "WWWWWWHHHHHHAAAAAAH!!!!" They found great joy in "whaaing" us as often as possible. The Brits were killing us with it.

Take a bunch of overachievers—guys who hate to lose—doing one of the most dangerous jobs on the planet, add a game that the majority of the Americans have never heard of, let alone played before, and it spells a recipe for a good time. Let the games begin. Before very long, the majority of the detail was having a blast. It got to the point where guys were afraid to answer any questions from anybody. Especially any questions coming from our British counterparts. They were the masters of the game and they abused us.

In a few short weeks, all the detail members were now up to speed and playing with any unwitting person they encountered in or around the CPA headquarters. No one was immune. This thing went viral over the course of weeks. In typical American fashion, the team took things to another level.

"Wow. Is that your M-4 you are carrying?"

"Yes."

"WHAAAAAH!"

To a guy standing outside the ambassador's office: "Are you waiting for the boss?"

"Yes."

"WHAAAAAH!"

To a guy in his gym clothes: "Nice shorts. Are you headed to the gym?"

"Yes."

"WHAAAAAH!"

It got annoying as hell.

The Brits may have shared the game with us, but things got out of control quickly. Fast-forward a few weeks and much of the detail was invited to the British ambassador's villa to have a few pints and rub elbows with a number of high-ranking British staff officials, including Ambassador Greenstock and the commanding general of all the British forces currently deployed in Iraq under the coalition banner. It was quite a party.

So as my guys are hanging out, the commanding general decides to address the assembled group. He started out with something to the effect of thanks for coming . . . blah, blah, blah . . . and then says: "We even have some of the Americans playing the 'whaah game.' We must stop this game immediately, as it's not proper manners. Are there any questions?"

Apparently the general did not realize that there were about twenty Americans in the crowd. Quickly a hand shoots up in the back of the crowed and Jadicus (former SEAL medic), one of my best smart-asses, says in his best British accent: "Sir, so what you are saying is there will be no more playing of the 'whaah game'?"

British general: "Why, yes, that is exactly what I'm saying . . ."

Before he could even finish his sentence, there was a loud and thunderous:

"Wwwwwwhhhhhhaaaaaaah!"

Needless to say the entire group, including the general, had a good chuckle. As I said, no one was immune.

Intel reports can be a great thing as evidenced above, but they can also drive you crazy. I had four separate entities bringing me valuable intelligence each day. Trying to decide what was actionable and should be shared with the team and what was pure rumor and not substantiated was a tough call. And, of course, getting to meet with these folks when they called was always difficult. They had full-time jobs and many others to brief. Including me daily was a pain in their ass. We rarely met in an office-type setting. The meetings would take place behind the palace, on the walkway to the gym, in the parking lot, outside my trailer, in the smoking area, or someplace else that could easily explain our "chance" meeting. And getting them to talk over the phone was nearly impossible. But without them, there is no telling how things might have turned out.

From the beginning I never wore body armor or carried a rifle when we were working in the Red Zone. As AIC I thought that I should present a more professional image and give the impression that extreme measures were not needed. But as the situation became more ominous and the intel reports more threatening, I began to occasionally wear my body armor and carry a rifle. When I did, my guys tensed up and wanted to know what I was not telling them. They clearly inferred I knew something that they did not. And they were correct. But as the leader of these guys my job was to keep them focused on their jobs and not over-load them with maybes, might-bes, or could-bes. They had to do their jobs each and every day regardless of the threats that were being made against the ambassador. We had a sign posted in the office that stated: THE BAD GUYS ONLY HAVE TO WIN ONCE; WE HAVE TO WIN EVERY DAY. That was our mind-set and focus. If we did our jobs properly each day, we would prevail and everyone would get home safely. End of story.

Around this time Scotty H came to my trailer one evening for a cold Heineken, and he told me that he had some bad news. He had been offered and had accepted a full-time gig with a government agency, and he was hoping to leave as soon as possible. FUCK. Scotty, by this time, had become my closest confidant and my most reliable asset, as well as being a damn good advance team leader. We talked about his replacement, and he said he thought that Sax was the best man for the job. A former SEAL with extensive spec-op experience, Sax was one of the smartest guys on the team. I asked Scotty to work with Sax so the transition would be as seamless as possible. He told me he already had started. That was Scotty—always a chess move ahead of everybody else. He left five days later.

My original thirty-six-man PSD team was again a thirty-four-man PSD team. Between the advance team, the detail team, the villa team, and now the door gunners, I was sweating each and every day. Who was sick, who was hurt, whose wife had just left him, whose kids were sick? Oh yeah, and did I mention the bad guys were going to kill us today? I had become the AIC, psychiatrist, scheduler, mother hen, and, according to some, the biggest asshole in Baghdad. I was juggling all the balls as fast I could. I had no patience for the weak, sick, lame, or lazy. I knew that

Blackwater's reputation was on the line (as well as mine), and I damn sure was not going to let either of us take a hit. I set a stern example and hoped the "real men" would follow suit. They did.

Of the thirty-four guys from the original rotation, about half were on sixty-day contracts and half on ninety-day contracts. This way, when the first group left and was replaced, they would have thirty days to learn the ropes from the ninety-day group, before the next group would arrive. It seemed like a good idea when it was first explained to me. The biggest problem was there was no real template on what we were doing and how we were doing it. Each day we changed some things around to make them better. Throwing in the helos with no training program for the pilots, the door gunners, or the tactical commander added another twist.

At no time did we ever have a quick reaction force (QRF) on standby to help us if we were attacked. Nor did we have the communications ability to call an SOS to other units in the Green Zone. Our radio base station at our own command post worked occasionally—if we were lucky. We did have cell phones, but there was no one there standing by ready to help us. Each day we went out it was just us and us alone. If we were attacked, the plan was for us to defend the ambassador and transfer him as quickly as possible to one of the helos and fly him out of the danger zone. The advance team would attempt to fight their way back to us, and hopefully everyone would survive. Not a great plan, but we had no other options. The MP CAT teams did have comms back to their unit, and we gave them one of our radios for each mission, but depending upon where we were and how long it would take them to get to us, it could be a while. The point is that there was nobody standing by if something horrific happened. It was just Frank and his merry band of Blackwater guys. The reality of this situation began to sink in with some of them. While everyone is brave and an ass-kicking machine when there is no real threat, the reality of pending death on every mission began to take a toll on some of the less-experienced guys. My Rangers, SEALs, Marines, Special Forces, and combat arms guys relished each mission. Some of the others? Yeah, not so much. I could see the stress mounting in a few of them. Despite the manpower issues, when a guy was not doing well, I tried to make sure he got a day off to decompress. Of course, he was then labeled as a weak link and I knew he would not be returning. Given the choice I would never knowingly allow a guy to come back if he had proven to me or the other leadership elements that he was a potential liability in any way, shape, or form. Big boy rules.

NOVEMBER 2003

As rotation time got closer I had a few guys come to me and ask if they could leave earlier than scheduled. I could see the stress and despair on their faces and listened to their stories of woe and distress back home. I knew some of them were not having fun. I learned later that some of them used these stories to break their contracts with Blackwater and jump ship to another company that was paying more. Other guys were in hog heaven and asked to extend and stay. Ken began the process of getting flights scheduled, and we waited for word on the incoming replacements we had been promised. Ken requested résumés and background information on each man so we could place them where we felt they would best fit as soon as they arrived. The résumés never came. We were often operating in a vacuum. Guys had contracts and wanted to leave on schedule. We did our best to process them. We had been promised that as each guy left, he would be replaced that day. It wasn't that smooth. While I was out with the ambassador, Ken kept working the arrival and departure flights, room assignments, gear, radios, and weapons inventories. He scrounged ammo and equipment and did all the paperwork to get the guys home and make sure they got paid. It was not easy.

Three guys got flights: thirty-four became thirty-one. Three more left and thirty-one became twenty-eight. We were still doing four or five missions every day. I cut back on the advance team and could only put a single shooter in each helo. We were severely shorthanded. As the AIC I took the brunt of the criticism from the team. Only Ken knew the true level of my frustration. I was so frustrated with the lack of support coming from Blackwater HQ back in Moyock that I had Ken regularly look at and edit my e-mails for a sanity check so I wouldn't come across as the complete fuming angry bastard I was.

"Ken, take a look at this e-mail. What do you think?"

"Frank, maybe 'you motherfuckers' isn't a good choice of words if you want them to actually answer you back and give you what we need."

"Yeah, you might be right."

We'd just laugh, and then Ken would rewrite it for me.

I put on the stern happy face and made sure everyone was focused on keeping the ambassador alive, but inside I was mad as hell. The hours were brutal. The villa team had been cut to four guys, and they were working twelve-hour shifts and then flying in the birds for four or five hours each day. I moved Shrek to the villa to run that side of the house. He was also flying and doing twelve-hour shifts. Single shifts at the office for an hour became multiple shifts every day. Everybody was pulling more than their weight, and I could see the stress was mounting. They knew as well as I did that we were not operating as efficiently as we should be. One thing about type A personalities is that you can't bullshit them, ever. And I did not try.

I called for a team meeting and I explained the situation. I was as honest as I could be. The truth was our replacements had been promised to us and were not inbound as of yet and from that day forward I told them no one else would be leaving until we got more guys. You could have heard a pin drop. The real men were like—"big fucking deal, we're getting paid, let's work." The guys who had promised their wives and kids that they wouldn't get killed were less than pleased. It sucked, but my hands were tied.

We got one new guy in. Now we had twenty-nine. People in the palace were beginning to notice that our numbers were down. When asked, I lied and said we were still fully staffed. Our contracting officer asked me to call for a full formation so he could count heads as he was sure I was full of shit. He was correct. I dodged. I zigged. I zagged. I blamed the operational tempo as the reason I never could hold the formation. I never did.

We pushed on. The forecasts of our demise kept coming, and the ambassador continued to do what he was doing. We continued to do what were supposed to do. There were no more excuses anymore for missing a day. If a guy was sick, I found something else for him to do.

One day I got a phone call from Blackwater HQ. I fully expected to hear that guys were inbound. Instead I was told that "someone" had conveyed to them tales of drunken debauchery, visits to whorehouses, fraternizing with females, and that the behavior had to stop. I nearly dropped the phone. Did the guys have a beer at the end of an eighteen-hour day? Absolutely. Were guys getting laid? Absolutely. Was there a whorehouse at the Al Rasheed? Hell no, there never had been, and besides the place had been closed for weeks at this time. I was beyond angry. They had to be kidding me. I was not, nor would I ever become the morality police. The big boy rules were in full effect. And they would stay in place. Not to mention there would have been a full-scale mutiny. The guys needed a way to decompress. It was a typical head shed move—deflect attention from what they were doing wrong and try to make the team play defense. It would never work. I knew how hard the guys were working, and the folks back in the States did not.

I asked about the replacements and was told they were working it and that I had to be patient. Great! I told them that no one else was leaving until the new guys were on a plane. They were not happy with me. And I was not happy with them. They were in danger of losing the contract and could not fathom it.

"If you want me to run this thing, let me run it; if not, find somebody else. The guys are busting their asses and risking their lives every day. We're understaffed. The folks in the palace know it, and you call me with this bullshit? Where are the armored vehicles we were promised? The automatic weapons? My ammo resupply? Don't waste my time with this fucking nonsense. People are going to get killed."

The next phone call was to ask me to stay another thirty days. I said yes. How could I leave when I was making others stay? Leadership from the front means holding yourself to as high or higher a standard than you hold everyone else. Thirty days had now become ninety days. The family was less than pleased, but if your country needs you to do something, you have to do it. Right? It was a crazy time.

The replacements finally began to arrive and it was like starting almost from scratch again. The stuff they were being taught in the train-up was not what we were doing on the ground. It was not their fault, but the Blackwater trainers had never been here. They were trying to guess how we were doing things. The experienced guys worked with the new guys to get them up to speed. The replacements wanted to test fire their weapons and zero them in. I had no ammo to do it. We had not had an ammo resupply, and any spare ammo that we did have had been used up by the first group when they'd zeroed their weapons. Guys asked about the armored vehicles they had been told they would drive, and I told them that what you see is what we have. They were not happy and some felt that they had been misled. I simply told them that I had never spoken to them before, so I had not misled them.

The Dirty 30 kept asking if they could use the birds to support some of their missions, so I called Brutus over to the palace one day and proposed a deal. I would let them use the birds if they supplied their own shooters and they gave me a couple of thousand rounds of ammo each time they used them. And they could only use them when the ambassador was going to be in his office for a minimum of three hours. That way, if the boss decided to move I could get the birds back in time to support their real job. I had become a pimp whoring out my flying bitches. Brutus agreed. I had made a deal I hoped and prayed would not bite me in the ass. I needed ammo; they needed air support.

I met with the pilots and explained what I had done. They were to call me as they took off, give me the grid coordinates of where they were headed, and call me when they returned. And I told them to make sure they counted the ammo before they took off. I also told them that there could be zero records, or any other reports, about what we were doing as the repercussions could sink Blackwater. Everyone agreed. Or so I thought. Apparently honor means nothing to a glory hound. One of the pilots had to thump his chest and write a report that got sent back to me from Blackwater with a WTF question mark.

Brian McCormick was one of my go-to guys from the ambassador's office. He had been instrumental in getting the Secret Service involved in the threat assessment for the ambassador and was by extension THE key reason Blackwater was given the contract. Brian had worked for Vice President Cheney, and after watching and working with the Secret Service at the White House and in Washington, D.C., he knew good security. He recognized that the ambassador was in jeopardy and he had started the assessment process by pointing out to his contacts in D.C. that there was the potential for a huge problem if the ambassador's security was not drastically improved—and improved quickly. Hence the arrival of the Secret Service assessment team in August. He was also honest to a fault. I could always trust him for a no-bullshit answer. And he was extremely bright. He had honestly felt that CID would get the ambassador killed. He had watched them for a few months and seen how they were doing things and compared this to his experience with the Secret Service.

Brian Mac now had begun to notice the new faces, and he asked me to explain why there were new people trying to learn a job that had been done well up to this point. I explained the rotation system that Blackwater was using. He was less than pleased and said the ambassador would not be happy. He reminded me that everyone else had signed up for a year and they were not rotating out. I nodded. I knew he was correct. I could not argue his point and said the decision was not mine. The next day he confirmed the ambassador's dismay at the development.

I called Blackwater to give them a heads-up about the prevailing thinking regarding the rotations. As usual, I was not taken seriously. They said that was how they were going to do it, end of story. Oh well.

About this time, the ambassador was summoned back to Washington for a meeting. We took him to the airport around midnight and waited until 0300 for the C-17 to arrive. It was loaded with military guys who had been wounded in action. The war was still raging in parts of Iraq. I had arranged with the ambassador's staff to try and get three of my guys on the plane to Andrews's air base if there was room. As luck would have it I was able to get all three on the plane. We got back to the palace around 0500, and everybody went to sleep for the first time in weeks without setting an alarm clock. I slept like a dead man. I woke up to my phone ringing. It was Ken telling that we had guys inbound and they would be here in a couple of hours. We mobilized a team to pick them up, and they arrived in time for evening chow.

That evening I organized a welcome aboard bash for the new guys, and an unwind-and-relax party for the guys who had been here. There was beer and Jack Daniel's for the men. About twenty-five of my guys were there, plus many of the British PSD guys, and some South Africans who were working on another detail; and generally anyone else who wanted to attend was welcome to swing by. At one point there had to have been close to a hundred people laughing and soaking in the chance to blow off some steam while the boss was away. The break was needed not just by us, but by everyone who was there.

The threats against the ambassador had escalated to direct threats against the Green Zone itself. There was a very credible threat to the palace area that ten teams of ten men would make a coordinated attack. The decision was made by someone at the

Department of Defense back in Washington, D.C., to replace the contracted Gurkha guards with a company of FAST Company Marines. (We often wondered if they were truly Gurkhas. The Gurkhas have a long and storied past as warriors. Some of these guys did not match that history in any way shape or form.) The Marines took control of the palace, placing teams of their men at all access points into the buildings and at all the entrances to the grounds. We welcomed this change of security. The FAST Company guys were no joke and took their orders and responsibilities extremely seriously. The fact that they were commanded by a former Marine Recon guy, Major Ottinger, made it even sweeter to me. They set up heavy-weapons emplacements, fortified fighting positions, and made the place a hell of a lot safer. It made keeping an eye on the ambassador at the palace a little less tense knowing that the Marines would be checking the IDs of all people coming in. It was a good thing. Their armorers even made repairs on a few of our weapons that were jacked up beyond the capability of Ken and our limited supply of weapons tools to fix. Semper Fi.

Up to this point, attacks on the palace grounds had been rare. The Iraqis had a curious habit of shooting into the air to celebrate almost anything, and the celebratory fire had punched holes in the some of the trailer roofs. A few people had been hit as the bullets eventually came back to Earth. I found more than a dozen bullets on the ground outside my trailer while I was there. I figured if my time was up, then it was up. I'm still not sure if you get into Valhalla if you're killed by celebratory fire, but we tried not to waste a lot of time or energy thinking about it. Guys on the team took to putting layers of three-quarter-inch plywood and sandbags on top of their trailers to stop the "what goes up, must come down" theory from providing them a late-night surprise.

On this particular evening things changed dramatically. Around 2100, over the music that was playing, we heard the unmistakable sound of a rocket being fired in our direction. We glanced up and saw it streaking overhead. Then came the tremendous explosion. The rocket had landed in the parking lot across the street from the palace and about 150 yards from the helos and pilots. A few of the pilots were with us. They immediately headed back to their billets for a head count and damage assessment. I had the shift leader and advance team leader account for their guys. No injuries to any of us. The new guys looked at me with a WTF expression. I shrugged and said, "Welcome to Baghdad." The rocket destroyed about fifty cars and left a pretty good sized hole in the ground where it landed. Fortunately no one was in the vicinity when it landed.

We thanked God, turned the music back on, and grabbed another drink. The party had dwindled to about fifteen folks at this time as many people, apparently way smarter than us, ran to the bunkers and hunkered down to wait for an all-clear command. We were Blackwater. We knew when our time was up we would not hear the explosion. We'd just get vaporized. So we partied on. The Marines came over and asked us to head inside for a few minutes while they checked on things. We did. Ten minutes later they announced the all clear, and the festivities resumed. Attacks became a part of the job. The type A personalities on the team always remained calm, cool, and collected—or at least pretended to even if we were not. Image is everything.

Soon the party numbers swelled back to well over a hundred. After the rocket attack it seemed like everyone needed a drink, and we always welcomed the company, especially the female company. By this time a Blackwater mystique had taken firm hold. We were the rock stars of the palace. And it certainly didn't hurt that the majority of the guys were built like professional athletes. The testosterone and strength oozed from their pores and they knew how to play the game. We were the superheroes keeping all the women safe. Or, at least, that's what we told anybody who would listen. The other guys rarely had a chance when it came to getting and keeping a female's notice. It was truly comical. Women got all the attention they could have imagined; they met guys who they would never have met back in the States; they had their choice of studs. What could be better? It was a good deal for all involved. The guys kept their stress levels reduced, and the women lived their fantasies. Everybody was happy.

These women were, by and large, extremely bright, professional career women—and aggressive. Most were college graduates with postgraduate degrees. Some were in politics, some were military, some were nurses and doctors, and some were career diplomats. They were smart as hell and knew what they wanted. I had great admiration for all of them. They were in the sandbox because they had volunteered to be there. They were driven to succeed to a degree rarely seen by most of us. And they endured the same discomfort and risks we did—the heat, the water outages, the power outages, the rocket and mortar attacks—and yet they showed up for work every day and they supported the mission to the best of their abilities. There was no crying in Baghdad. Some of them were tougher than some of my guys. They were truly a breath of fresh air. And they smiled and smelled a lot better than did my guys.

The new guys were quickly brought onto the teams in positions that I thought best met their backgrounds and skill set. It was a trying process. Without any résumés to review, placing guys was difficult. Ken had to get a quick feel for them, and then we hoped the new guys had not misled us about their past. Some did. The reaction to the new members of the team by the experienced members was always difficult to manage. The margin for error was nonexistent by this point. We were running 100 mph each and every day. The new guys were expected to pull their weight immediately, and the guys who had been here for a while were very quick to point out any and all mistakes. Several times each day, someone would come to me and tell me how this guy or that guy was not going to make it. The experienced guys knew what the risks were, the new guys did not. I urged each complainer to work with the new man, and told him to try to remember that only a few short weeks ago he himself did not know his ass from a hole in the ground. Tempers were short.

More than once guys had to be separated after exchanging words. New guys did not know what they did not yet know. Guys who had been there knew what the risks were and knew why we did things certain ways. The good-idea fairy is a dangerous thing in a war zone. I begged the new guys to learn *our way* for at least thirty days before they came up with suggestions we had already tried and likely eliminated weeks or months earlier. We did what worked, not what we thought might work. We were writing the book, not reading it.

The story that the new guys were being told back in Moyock and the promises they were being given by Blackwater HQ during the train-up created frustration and disenchantment when these guys realized immediately they were not being issued the gear and not being assigned to the team leader slot that someone back home had promised. OOOPs! Not my problem. My only promise was that once they got to the sandbox we would work them to death. Maybe not in the spot they wanted, but the spot we thought they could best fill.

Another intel report came in stating that a raid had uncovered videotape and photos of the detail at various locations we had been to with the ambassador. We always assumed the bad guys had been doing surveillance on us, but it had never been confirmed until this point. Surveillance is always an important part of the bad guys' arsenal. They wanted and needed to know how we were operating, our tactics and techniques, so they could attack us in a way that would maximize their chances of success. Everywhere we went there were photographers, press, and others milling about taking pictures. Who were the bad guys? Hell, we had no idea. This information caused me to pause and reflect on how we were doing our job. Should we change anything? If so, what and how? With new guys arriving it went without saying that many times people were out of position, and the synergy of fill and flow was not what it had been with the guys who had been working together for weeks.

The press is the bane of any protection operation's existence. They were difficult to work with at best. Al Jazeera had a bad habit of being on the scene minutes before spectacular attacks took place against coalition forces and personnel, and was thus able to record and broadcast the mayhem. Was the press doing research for the bad guys? I went to our press team to see if we could somehow limit or restrain the press at certain events. It was then I learned that from a public figure's point of view, if an event is not recorded and broadcast, it never took place. It was a sobering realization that everything we did was going to be recorded, and that the press would be an integral aspect of anything that happened. We had a job to do and so did they. We had to work together.

I met with Sax and we decided the press would have to get to the locations at least an hour before the boss did so that we could check their equipment for explosives, weapons, etc. Then we would confiscate their cell phones so they could not call anyone to let them know exactly when the ambassador would be arriving. We kept them sequestered in a holding area and assigned a guy from the advance team to keep an eye on them. Individuals found videotaping outside the location had their cameras taken from them and held until after the detail team had departed. This was not met with any enthusiasm from the press corps, but we had to do what we had to do, while they were doing what they had to do. It was a compromise that neither side was happy with.

As the new guys settled in, the remaining members of the first group began to make noises about their pending departures. I was faced with the realization that in a few short weeks I would have an entirely new crew working with me. The prospect of that did not make me happy. It seemed that every time things were going smoothly, a new problem popped up. Unfortunately for me, Ken was also scheduled to depart. This meant that his sidekick would have to make all the arrangements for the guys leaving and the guys coming in. I asked Ken to take his partner under his wing and make sure that he had a full and solid grasp of how to make these things happen.

One morning around 0630, while waiting for the ambassador to come out of the villa, I got a call on my radio that there was something that I just had to see. I headed out to the parking area and saw my stone-cold-killer PSD team standing there staring up in the sky.

"Can you believe this?"

"Oh my God, I never thought we'd see them again."

"Wow."

My guys were staring at clouds. There had been zero clouds since I arrived in August, and now floating peacefully in the Iraqi sky there they were. It was quite a sight, especially when a group like this was staring, slack-jawed, at Mother Nature. It's the little things that sometimes make for a good day. In hindsight I can remember it raining only twice the entire time I was there. Both times for about twenty minutes. The clouds were cool.

Early on another morning, I got a call from the "Force Protection" commander (a Marine major in charge of overall security for the palace grounds); he asked me if one of my guys had
an accidental discharge at the airport PX the day before. An accidental discharge occurs when someone fires his or her weapon
when the person is not expecting it to go off. It is also referred to
by professionals as a negligent discharge because if you are carrying a weapon there are no accidents, just negligence. I responded
that I had not heard anything about it but would look into it.

I called the advance team and detail team leaders over to my
trailer, and asked them if they knew anything about this. They
did. And, of course, had hoped that I would never catch wind of
it. With around forty-six guys now on the ground it was impossible for me to be everywhere at all times, and I relied upon the
different group leaders to keep me in the loop. I was pissed. It
seems that one of the new guys had tried to unload his Glock
before entering the PX and had managed to squeeze off a round
into the clearing barrel. This guy was a former SEAL who had
been brought over to my team after a stint with The Dirty 30.
He had been described as a weapons expert, weapons instructor,
sniper, and a great guy by their team leader. I had found it odd;
if he was all that and a bag of chips, why had they let him go? I
soon found out.

I called Blackwater and told them I was sending another guy
home. As a SEAL-centric organization, the leaders at Blackwater
were very protective of their brother SEALs. I was soon to find
out just how protective they were, and how protective they had
been. Ken managed to get this guy a plane ride out the next day

and off he went. I hated losing another guy, but Blackwater and my reputation were at stake here. A negligent discharge is unacceptable anywhere in the world. It was even truer in a war zone. We were supposed to be the best of the best, and this incident gave us a huge black eye. I was now asked repeatedly about my "high-speed, low-drag superninja operators."

At the chow hall the next day I ran into several of my friends from The Dirty 30. They had heard what had happened, and they were enjoying my pain immensely. They could not understand why I had even agreed to take him after what had happened to him on their team. I had no idea what they were talking about. I said I had heard nothing but great things about him from their team leader and Blackwater HQ. It seems as though this guy had a negligent discharge while he was with them and had actually shot himself in the leg. I was stunned. The light came on very quickly that I had been played like a fool by Blackwater. They had apparently hoped I would never find out, and that the guy would somehow save his reputation by working on The Bremer Detail. I was beyond pissed off. Needless to say, I exchanged some unpleasantries with their team leader, and from that day forward their access to my helos was severely limited. As long as that particular team leader was there, they could not use them. Fool me once, shame on you; fool me twice, shame on me. I could no longer trust him, and I never did again.

As though I did not have enough other things to occupy my time, a few days later another memo about drinking in-country and fraternizing with women came down the wire from Blackwater HQ. This was getting ridiculous. I knew where this was coming from, but could never prove it. I posted the memo without comment, and I never mentioned it again. I don't even know if the guys read it. The funny part is, just two days before this we had attended a party with the Dirty 30 guys. They had a bar set up at their place where they served drinks to any and all.

We had made a run out to the airport to pick someone up and had decided to stop by and say hello. As we approached the Dirty 30 camp we could see flames soaring forty feet into the air. They had strung Christmas lights up, and the music was blasting. On the walls of some buildings, .50 caliber machine gun impact holes etched out their familiar pattern. It was like a scene from the old *Apocalypse Now* movie. There were two hundred people gyrating to the flames and under the lights. It was surreal. Every few minutes somebody would throw another pallet on the fire and the flames kept rising. The highlight of the evening was when one of the female attendees actually fell ass first into the fire. Fortunately she was not badly burned. So, somehow, these guys could operate a bar, but we could not have a beer. They could light women on fire, but we couldn't fraternize with our female colleagues and coworkers. What was the deal? Apparently, according to them, they were never questioned about their after-hour activities. The HQ hypocrisy was overwhelming.

As the party wound down it became time to head back to the Green Zone. It was about 0200, and we had to navigate the airport road. The prime time to be attacked traveling this stretch of highway was just after dark to dawn. The Iraqis would wait for dark to set up their ambushes and wait for the first unsuspecting coalition convoy to happen upon it. It could be an IED attack, a small-arms ambush, or an attack from vehicles lying in wait. They used the darkness to their advantage and they were very good at what they did. We were leaving in the prime attack hours. Q was driving one vehicle, a level-6 armored monster with a 500-hp McLaren engine. Travis T was in a Suburban. As we moved out onto the highway the speeds went up dramatically. Our best ally was speed, and speed is what we did. The best we could hope for was to throw off the timing of any possible attack. We wanted to blow past the IEDs that were waiting for us before the bad guys could react. Q was at 120 mph before I knew it. I was just along for the ride. The bad guys would have had to be extremely good to hit us. As we rounded the last overpass for the final stretch home the tires were chirping from the speed. We made it back safe and sound.

We continued to work our asses off. The ambassador, we had become convinced, was a cyborg. He never got tired. He just kept going. He had a trip being organized to Spain. I notified Blackwater we had a pending international trip, and I began (or rather Ken began) the process of gun permits, visas, hotel rooms, etc. Everything was in motion when Blackwater called me and told me that international trips were not part of our contract with DOD. This was not my fight, so I approached Brian Mac. The DOD rep said yes, we were expected to provide protection for him anywhere he went with the exception of the United States. Okay . . . we continued to plan. Blackwater came back and said no, we would not be going. This back-and-forth took place over the next twenty-four hours before Blackwater finally confirmed we would be going. I began to question my own sanity. I had never seen the contract, so I had no idea who was right or wrong when it came to contractual issues.

I chose six guys to go. The six had been around since the beginning of September; and I felt it was a good way for them to relax, eat some decent chow, and get a taste of real life for a few days before they rotated home. I would stay behind and train with the new guys.

Our away team had been in Spain for about a day when the ambassador was called back to the United States. This concerned me, as I was always fearful of the guys not having any adult supervision. My fears were not unfounded. There really is no way that what happened could have been much worse. It was a disaster.

In Baghdad we trained, went to the gym, took long-needed naps. After evening chow, Ski and I decided to relax and have a couple of drinks. Ski had been there since the beginning and was a great guy. About 2200 hours my cell phone rang. It was Ambassador Pat Kennedy, Bremer's chief of staff, telling me to come immediately to his office. My heart sank. I knew this could not in any way, shape, or form be good. Ski and I headed straight over, and Ambassador Kennedy was in his office with Colonel Sabol. This was going to be way worse than I had imagined. Sweat soaked my shirt.

Ambassador Kennedy was Ambassador Bremer's right-hand man. He was a career diplomat who had been in charge of the Diplomatic Security Service for a period of time. He was a no-nonsense, straight shooter of the highest order. He had been a key ally of mine during the start-up phase of the Blackwater operation and had gone way beyond the call of duty to make sure we had whatever we needed to keep Ambassador Bremer safe. I liked him and respected him. He was smart and never asked a question to which he did not already know the answer. The conversation began: "Frank, if a member of your team assaulted a member of President Bush's staff, what would you do?"

"Sir, I would fire him."

"Frank, if this happened in Spain, what would you do?"

"Sir, as soon as he got back, I'd have him on a plane out of here."

"Frank, do you think there are any flights directly from Spain to the United States?"

"Yes, Sir, I'm sure there are."

"Frank, is there any good reason for bringing him back here instead of putting him on the next flight to JFK?"

"None that I can think of, Sir."

"Good, can you arrange that tonight?"

"Yes, Sir, I will."

"Good, have a great evening"

"You too, Sir."

Fuck me. I got ahold of Ken and Blackwater, and we started the process. I got ahold of the guys in Spain and asked what had happened. Apparently after the boss departed, the party lamp had been lit. Two days of cavorting had led to two of the six guys being late for departure to the airport to board the C-130 back to Baghdad. When questioned as to why they were late, the individual in question (a former Marine, still drunk) got a tad surly with a member of the president's staff. When further pressed as to the reason for being late, the guy asked the man if he knew what the capital of Thailand was. The man hesitated for a second, and my guy punched him square in his nut sack and yelled, "BANGKOK!" This can be funny in the proper setting, but this clearly was not the proper setting. The fight was on. Punches were thrown and the Spanish cops had to stop the fight. Cooler heads prevailed, and the president's men declined to have the Spanish police arrest my guy. Thank God.

I assigned two guys (Riceman and Tony T) to keep him in his room, telling them to stand by for instructions. If the incident wasn't bad enough, this idiot had failed to check his weapon into the weapons box with all the other guns, so I now had a drunk guy in Spain with a gun. I did not know how I would get the weapon back to Iraq. Even getting the two guys who were babysitting back to Iraq was going to be tough. Fuck.

The guy called me crying and sobbing hysterically and accusing me of not having his back. "Frank, what are you doing to me?"

"You're going home tomorrow."

"I didn't do anything."

"You smacked a member of the president's staff."

"It wasn't my fault."

"Doesn't matter. You did it. Big boy rules. Have a safe flight home."

"I can't believe you're fucking me over like this."

"You did it. You own it."

"It's not fair."

Whatever.

The next day he was gone. Ken and one of the other guys packed up his luggage and found some missing gear from the detail, including a $14,000 set of night vision goggles that was apparently going to find its way to his home when he left. They shipped his kit back to the States minus the almost-stolen gear. My guys took the illegal weapon to the embassy where Bill Miller had arranged for the regional security officer (RSO) in charge of the security at the U.S. embassy in Spain to somehow get it shipped back to Baghdad. It took my guys four days to return. The weapon arrived a month later. In the meantime, since we still had a mission to meet and were one gun short, Ken had to give up his own sidearm so one of the new detail guys would be armed while out with the ambassador.

Ambassador Kennedy never mentioned the incident again. That's the kind of man he was. Problem solved. Move on.

The rotation of the men continued to be an issue for the ambassador and his staff. They were none too pleased as the newer guys continued to make the same elementary mistakes that the earlier guys had made and had stopped making. I did not blame them. It was making me crazy also. How many phone calls can you get about the same mistakes being made over and over? Again I notified Blackwater that this was an issue. Again I got the "shut up and color" speech. Blackwater did not like to hear constructive criticism, and I think they wished that I would stop questioning them or giving them a heads-up on anything. They would have been far happier if I sat in the corner with a box of crayons and a coloring book. All I could do was to try and keep everybody happy.

One of our ongoing challenges was that we frequently had folks from D.C. visiting. It was far from unusual. For example, around this time, November 2003, Jim Cawley, one of the Secret Service guys who had done the original assessment, came back to Baghdad to "arrange" security for a pending visit from Senators Hillary Clinton and Jack Reed, and to see what and how we were doing. The senators were supposedly heading to Baghdad after a stop in Afghanistan. Jimmy Cawley was a great guy. He came over to the villa and inspected the improvements they had recommended and we had made to the ambassador's primary residence, and we reviewed the tactics and techniques that we were employing. He told me if I ever had any issues to contact him directly, and he would contact the director of the Secret Service to make sure we got any and all support we required. The Blackwater contract was under tremendous scrutiny back in Washington. As the threats came in, all parties involved knew we could not fail. We had his full backing.

Thanksgiving morning, Brian called me to the office saying the ambassador needed to speak with me. Later in the day we were scheduled to accompany the ambassador to a USO show at Baghdad International Airport. Midafternoon my advance team would be heading out to BIAP to begin the security preparations for our arrival. I walked into the office, and the ambassador asked me if I had set up security for the event. I told him the advance team would be heading over shortly. He said we should stand by and not head out there just yet as President Bush would be arriving and the Secret Service was there setting up the security. I almost fell over. He smiled and asked me if I was okay with the Secret Service taking the lead on this one. I replied through a smile that I thought they could handle it. He told me that I was now the third person at the palace to know about it.

I called the detail leader and the advance team leader to my trailer and I told them to stand down. I advised them that for today we would not have the lead for security at the event. They looked at me like I had lost my damn mind. I said, "Trust me. When you get out there, just follow the directions from whoever you run into." They did.

The Secret Service directed the advance team to take a position fairly close by, but not close enough to be in their way. When the ambassador arrived, I was allowed in along with one other guy from our team. They asked if we were armed, we said we were, and in a huge show of respect they allowed us to keep our weapons. In the world of the Secret Service, they rarely if ever let anyone not part of their team carry a weapon around the president. It was a good day.

The president arrived and met the ambassador, and they talked for a few minutes before the president marched into the mess hall to a huge ovation. I got goose bumps. Here was the president of the United States in Baghdad, serving Thanksgiving dinner to the troops. It was truly a moment I will never forget. The Secret Service guys were as professional as they always are. We exchanged a few words, and Jimmy Cawley introduced me to the director of Protective Operations for the Secret Service, and a few other heavy hitters who were in attendance. Mark Sullivan told me again that if we ever need anything not to hesitate to call. I certainly knew I would if I had to. Eventually, in May, I would have to make that call when problems arose with some of our military counterparts.

6 DECEMBER 2003

On a Red Zone run several days later, Ambassador Bremer came out of his meeting with Secretary of Defense Donald Rumsfeld and the head of the Islamic Supreme Council of Iraq Abdul Aziz al-Hakim, at Hakim's house in Baghdad, and turned to me and said he would be going to the airport with the secretary of defense. This was not part of my detailed plan for the day. We had expected to head directly back to the Green Zone and the palace. My initial reaction was to protest the move, but I could see from the look in his eyes that this was not open for debate. I answered "Yes, Sir" and relayed the information to the team.

The road to BIAP was referred to in many ways—none of them favorable. We usually called it the highway of death, as the insurgents repeatedly targeted and killed coalition forces making the dangerous journey between the airport and the Green Zone. Adrenaline pumped as I made a mental checklist of items we had not been able to do to make this trip as safe as possible: no advance team; no helicopter briefing; the route had not been cleared; no idea/intel of events that had occurred on Route Irish that day.

Many major components of a regular mission were not in place. The flip side was that, as this was an unscheduled visit, no one knew we were heading out there, and we would be traveling with the additional manpower and firepower that accompanied Secretary Rumsfeld. I notified the team that there had been a change in plans and that we were off to the VIP lounge at the airport. Needless to say, some of the radio traffic back to me expressed grave concern about doing the mission, à la "Are You Nuts?!"

The twenty-minute trip out to the airport was uneventful. However, the eighteen or so car motorcade with U.S. Army Apache helicopters, Kiowa helicopters, and my two Little Birds certainly told everyone in the area something unusual and noteworthy was taking place at the airport this evening. Imagine eighteen-plus vehicles moving as if controlled by one mind. We called it "the motorcade dance." All were moving within mere feet of each other. All were rolling at 60–70 mph. It was a thing of beauty. We arrived safely, and the meeting began.

I gathered my men and explained that getting back to the Green Zone was going to be an adventure, and to make sure that everyone was aware of the dangers—a truly unnecessary step as they all knew the risks. While we had the advantage of surprise on our way *to* the airport, this would be lost on the return. We should expect a lot of unwanted attention on the way back. We laughed and said our good-byes to one another and promised to have a cup of mead in Valhalla later that evening. One has to love the macabre sense of humor among security contractors.

At 2320 the meeting broke up. Ambassador Bremer and Brian McCormick came out, and we loaded them into the motorcade.

We were the first motorcade to leave that evening, and the irony of being the advance motorcade heading down the highway of death was not lost on any of us. Earlier, because we had had no idea how long we would be there, I had told Hacksaw to have the Little Birds land at the airport and stay with us. I could not risk having the ambassador come out, and us not having the helos. Our adrenaline levels spiked. It was late. And very dark. The Little Birds were in the air flying top cover and scanning for potential issues. Due to manpower issues I had only one shooter in each bird, Shrek and another guy.

We had two up-armored Humvees working as our lead CAT element in front of the protection detail motorcade. Our lead car, driven by Travis T had Riceman sitting in the front-right seat working as the tactical commander. Behind him we had two additional shooters staring intently out the windows peering into the darkness looking for potential problems. The limo had Q behind the wheel, and I was sitting in the front-right seat with the ambassador directly behind me. Brian Mac was sitting behind Q. The follow car had a driver, and Ski sitting right front acting as the shift leader. Behind them were two more shooters watching their areas of responsibility, and behind them in the third seat we had Doc Jones. Following up as rear security were two more up-armored CAT vehicles.

From my position in the limo, a level-6 armored SUV, I could watch Q at the wheel and Hacksaw flying lead helo above. As we progressed, Hacksaw reported a suspicious vehicle backing down an on-ramp on the highway. He radioed that he was going to fly over and check it out. The shift leader gave the command to shift the limo to the left (away from the side of the road and away from the entrance to the on-ramp and toward the center median) while the follow and lead cars shifted to the right.

Seconds later all hell broke loose.

I heard something hit my window. While I was trying to figure out what it was there was an explosion of light and sound. The limo veered. Q fought to retain control. Temporarily blinded by the explosions we could see nothing. I leaned over the seats to check on the ambassador and Brian just as the ambassador asked what had happened. "Bomb and AK fire, Sir," I told him. Despite the sound of the explosions, we could still hear AKs being fired at us. I asked the boss if he was okay, and he confirmed he was. I could see the back of the limo had sustained severe damage (the rear window was gone, and the door itself was bent), and I directed him and Brian to get down. Despite the damage, Q was firmly in control of the vehicle. The bad guys were shooting at the limo as we sped away at roughly 60 mph through the smoke-induced fog. Neither Q nor I could see anything more than five feet in front of us. Q was driving purely by instinct and training.

Over the radio I heard the shift leader, Ski, calling out, "TUNA, TUNA, TUNA"—our code to drive directly through an ambush, getting off the "X" and out of the kill zone. The smoke cleared and I looked to my right to see the follow car driver about twenty-four inches away from me using his car to shield the limo—his side mirror touching Q's side mirror at 60 mph. I asked for a casualty report and learned that two of our four CAT team vehicles were damaged, but limping along. No injuries to any of the detail or CAT team members.

As all this was happening, Ambassador Bremer leaned over and casually asked Brian Mac, "Tell me again why we shouldn't go to Davos?" They had been discussing the upcoming trip to Davos when the attack happened. And in typical Bremer fashion. He never panicked, just went right back to the subject at hand.

As the AIC I had to make the painful decision that the damaged CAT vehicles were on their own. I was unsure of the damage to the limo, and the ambassador's safety always came first.

The shift leader radioed me again to ask if we were all right. I responded, "That's an affirm." Apparently the damage to the limo was far greater than I realized. The follow car guys could see it, we couldn't. We were advised to slow our vehicle down to make sure we reached the Green Zone safely. Q throttled back to about 45 mph. And we made it back.

Inspecting the damage to the motorcade vehicles after arrival we found several bullet holes in the rear of the lead vehicle. The limo had lost the back end (the nonarmored hatch area), the electronic countermeasure (ECM) device had been destroyed, and we found shrapnel and bullet holes in the armored area just behind the rear seats where the ambassador and Brian had been sitting. The ECM blocks radio and telephone signals from being able to set off explosive devices. The IED must have been command detonated, meaning that, rather than being radio controlled, it was hardwired to explode when the terrorist pressed a button to initiate the device. In hindsight we concluded we had happened upon the ambush site before the insurgents had finished their nasty surprise for us. They must have shot at us hoping that we would slow down or stop and engage them. There were additional bullet holes in the right side of the car and, of course, one that was even with my head on my window. The follow car had extensive shrapnel damage and bullet holes riddling the body. When the explosion went off the heat from the blast convinced both the shift leader and the driver their feet had been badly burned. Fortunately it had been only painful, not permanent. Fifteen minutes later the CAT vehicles finally limped in. All the tires had been destroyed and they had sustained extensive shrapnel damage.

The ambassador took a look at the car and asked again if everyone was okay. I said we were all fine. He turned and walked to his office and went right back to work. I met with Dan Senor, spokesman for the Coalition Provisional Authority (CPA), who asked if the incident would be on the news. I told him there was no way we would be reporting it. The ambassador called me to his office, and we talked about keeping the incident quiet and whether he should mention it to his wife or not. I told him he might want to mention it because this way if she heard about it, she would know he was safe.

Minutes later I got a call from Brutus telling me that one of the Dirty 30 teams had been attacked on the road, and that they heard sounds of an attack about fifteen minutes before their guys had been hit. I told him the first attack had been against us. Our convoy to the airport had drawn a lot of attention.

I notified Blackwater that we had been hit but suffered no casualties. They thanked me for the briefing. I also called Jimmy Cawley from the Secret Service and gave him the details. I knew the Secret Service would want to know the details firsthand and not through the media, if news of the attack became public. He was thankful that no one was hurt and that Bremer was safe.

Somehow, the news didn't leak out for two weeks. Who leaked it, I still do not know. Someone in Washington spilled it to the D.C. press. Very quickly everyone knew about it, and the Iraqi press pressured the ambassador for his reaction. He calmly stated it had happened two weeks earlier and it had not altered or changed the way he did his job or how he conducted his business as evidenced by the schedule that he had maintained since the incident. Dan Senor added at a press conference that the ambassador had full faith in his security team to keep him safe. There were some family members of guys on the team who were not happy when they heard about it, but we had all survived. No harm, no foul.

In retrospect I'm still not sure who the bad guys thought they were attacking or why no one ever took credit for the attack. The mission to the airport had been unscheduled but extremely high profile, so I think we were just a target of opportunity. Wrong place, wrong time.

That night, after making my calls, I had headed over to Blackwater Boulevard to check on the guys. It was by then about 0100.

Me: "Everybody OK?"

The team, all talking at once: "Damn, that was close."

"Those motherfuckers."

"Have a drink."

"How's the boss?"

"Shit, they almost got us."

And on it went for about thirty minutes. I trudged back to my trailer and tried to sleep. The adrenaline was slowly wearing off, and my thoughts were filled with the usual thousand "what if" questions. I finally dozed off.

We found out the next day that the IED consisted of eight howitzer shells wired together. Only the first two had gone off. The six that had not exploded were placed in our direction of travel. In other words, as we drove away from the first explosion we were meant to roll right over another three times more powerful! Thank God the guys who wired it had made a mistake, and that we were moving fast, otherwise the results would have been different. One more of our nine lives had been used up. How many more did we have left?

Two days after the attack Blackwater notified me that my replacement and some other new guys would be arriving the following week. I knew this news was not going to be well received by the ambassador. I told Blackwater that their post-attack timing could not be worse. They told me to tell him, and "to make it work." Yeah, right. They still did not realize that we were on the ground and knew more than they did back in Moyock, North Carolina. No matter how many times we tried to make them understand the ground truth reality of what was going on, they lived in some fantasy world where they were far smarter than we were. I talked to Ken and he just shook his head and said good luck.

I called Brian and requested an appointment with Ambassador Bremer. Brian asked what was up, and I told him what the Blackwater plan was. He expressed total shock and asked me if I had been telling Blackwater about the issues with the rotations, and how they had not been sitting well with anybody on the ambassador's staff. I told him I had. He said he would get back to me. Usually when I requested time with the ambassador, unless it was a true emergency, I would have a few hours before he could slot me in. Ten minutes later the phone rang. It was Brian telling me the boss wanted to see me now.

I walked into the office and could tell by the looks I was getting that this would not be pleasant. Brian immediately ushered me in to see the ambassador. Again, way out of the norm. I usually had time for a coffee and some chitchat with Sue Shea, Bremer's executive assistant. Not this time.

Brian: "Sir, Frank is here."

"Frank, Brian tells me that you're leaving next week."

"Sir, this is what Blackwater told me today."

"Why? Everyone else is doing a year here."

"Blackwater thinks rotating guys in and out is a good idea."

"I want you to stay as long as I'm here. Are you okay with that?"

"Sir, I can only do what Blackwater tells me to do."

"Are you on a DOD contract?"

"Yes, Sir."

"Good, I'll call SecDef Rumsfeld right now."

With visions of Blackwater getting kicked out of country, I said: "Sir, I'm not sure it needs to go to that level."

He paused for a second and said: "Get Colonel Sabol in here right now."

I grabbed my phone, called Colonel Sabol, and told him the ambassador wanted to see him right away. He asked what was up, and as I was in the office and could not talk I said just get here ASAP.

The colonel arrived within five minutes, went into the ambassador's office, then came out and told me he would take care of it. And he did. About ninety minutes later he called and said I was not leaving. I asked him what had happened. He said he called Blackwater and asked to speak to Erik Prince or Gary Jackson. He was told they were not available. He said they had sixty minutes to call him back or he was calling the SecDef. When asked why, he told the lady on the phone what was in play. Ten minutes later they called back and said I would not be replaced. Mr. Prince clearly understood that the client, especially this client, is always right when it comes to how he wanted the contract supported, and who he wanted with him.

Almost everybody on the team was happy I would not be leaving. My wife and kids were not as happy as the team. Thirty days had now been extended to an undetermined time period. In a weird way I was extremely excited to be seeing this through to the end. The ambassador had paid me a huge compliment and had given me a huge endorsement. I felt good that apparently all the stuff I had been juggling and dealing with was really worth the time and effort. Blackwater, on the other hand, wasn't quite as happy as they made out to be on the phone with the ambassador's staff. I got a call from Blackwater HQ later that day and was basically accused of leveraging my relationship with the ambassador so I could stay in the country and make more money. Of course, the ambassador had nothing to do with this decision, as I had apparently brainwashed him and it was not that we were doing an excellent job. We hadn't just survived a fairly sophisticated assassination attempt, had we? Once again, Blackwater HQ was out of touch with the ground truth, and was trying to run the show from the safety of their office trailer in Moyock.

At this time I learned that the majority of my e-mail communication was not being passed along to everyone who should be seeing it at Blackwater HQ. Apparently a few members of the division had been kept in the dark about some of my concerns and did not know that the ambassador had expressed concern about the rotations and other issues. From this point forward I copied everyone on the e-mails. Fool me once, shame on you; fool me twice, shame on me. And magically a lot of my problems disappeared. Imagine that.

A couple of days later we headed to Bahrain with the ambassador so he could watch the Iraqi national soccer team continue in their quest to compete in the 2004 Olympic Games. My advance team, which had departed two days earlier, met us at the airport. We went to the hotel to check in. I could tell by their smiling faces that my guys had done their work, then had an evening or two of relaxation. We went to the game, then to a dinner, and finally back to the hotel. Ski had arranged for a couple of the advance team guys to watch the ambassador while Ski took me out to dinner and for a drink. He was always looking out for my mental health. We arrived at an establishment that had been scouted out the night before by the advance team guys.

Festus and a few of the other guys were already there. They were relaxing and admiring the menu, which seemed to consist primarily of young Thai ladies. Festus was a former SEAL who was one of the funniest guys I have ever met. He was a great shooter and could always be relied upon for moments of hilarity. This particular evening I witnessed something I had never seen before. Festus ordered a shot of some liquor. A few young lovelies had been trying to win his heart for the evening. He was fighting them off as best he could. Out of the blue he stood up, dropped his pants, dunked the head of his dick into the shot glass, then grabbed his lighter and lit his dick on fire. Had I not seen it with my own eyes I would not have believed it. Then he downed the shot and pulled his pants back up. Needless to say, he got quite an ovation from the other patrons. And because it was funny once, it became a recurring performance throughout the rest of his tour with us. Boys will be boys.

The word spread quickly through the team I would not be leaving and morale really picked up. It seemed as though rumors of my departure and the speculation on my replacement had made a lot of the guys nervous. They had seen the attempts at controlling the show and the Monday morning quarterbacking from North Carolina. And they feared that the wheels would come off the machine that we had created together. If you were not working with the team, you truly could not have any idea of the stress, or the hoops we constantly jumped through. The guys knew I was protecting both them and the ambassador. The Marine Corps adage—accomplish the mission and look out for the welfare of your men—rang true with me every day we were there. The guys knew I could be stern, but I always tried to be fair.

Ken rotated out and handed the Ops/support responsibilities to his assistant. Apparently Ken had overestimated his sidekick's grasp of how things were done. We rotated three more guys out and for some reason they were sent to Kuwait instead of Amman. The new Ops/support guy did not realize (read: failed to do his homework) that the guys would need visas before arrival into Kuwait as opposed to simply buying them at the customs counter upon arrival as we were able to do in Jordan. The three guys were quickly placed under house arrest while I attempted to sort the fiasco out. I did not get much sympathy from the Air Force colonel who was in charge of flights. He was beyond pissed off that we had screwed this up. His counterpart in Kuwait was threatening to send the guys back to Baghdad. And, of course, it was entirely my fault.

Further compounding the problem was that one of the guys was a Swiss citizen traveling on a Swiss passport. We called him Hillbilly because he was anything but: he was a former French Foreign Legion guy who spoke five languages and could fly a helicopter in addition to having extensive protection experience. He had a great skill set and was a good man. I'd met him ten years earlier at a school we both had attended.

However, the U.S. embassy in Kuwait could not do much to help him. Once again I had to go hat in hand to Ambassador Kennedy and ask for help in a situation that was embarrassing as hell and, in my mind, made us look stupid. He arranged visas for the two Americans, but said Hillbilly was going to be a little bit more difficult. The Americans finally left three days later, but Hillbilly ended up doing seven days under house arrest before he was allowed to leave. I knew that if Hillbilly ever ran into this Ops/support guy again that he would have killed him. Fortunately, they never crossed paths, as I made the decision that Ken's assistant would never come back. Hillbilly did come back after his scheduled home leave rotation.

The new arrivals were actually better than some of the original team members. By now Blackwater had had more time to recruit and train. These new guys quickly became the backbone of the team for the rest of the mission. The other good thing was that nearly 75 percent of them continued to extend so they were never replaced. Jimmy Dog, Mongo, Q, Travis T, HB, Carmine, Drew B, Sax, G-Money, Jadicus, Matt B, Jeremy W, Riceman, Billy C, Russ T, Gino N, and a few others had become the guys on whom I could always rely. Blackwater balked a few times at letting them stay past their rotation dates, but finally stopped fighting me about it. Most times, if they wanted to stay, they did. Things were looking up.

The next week, five guys arrived in-country. Among them were B-Town, one former Marine, two more former SEALs, and the guy designated as my replacement. Unbeknownst to me these guys had all been promised leadership slots to run the show after I left. They got settled in, and I sensed there were some problems bubbling beneath the surface. B-Town tracked me down and explained what had happened. Apparently none of these guys had been told I was not leaving. I had already slotted B-Town to take over the advance team, as he had previously run it for two months when he worked with the CID guys back in the beginning. Unfortunately one of the other former SEALs thought this was going to be his job.

I had a meeting with each of the guys and told them they were welcome to stay, but they would start at the entry-level positions and learn the job just like everybody else. There was no way I was going to put the ambassador in jeopardy, nor the team, while these guys tried to learn where the chow hall was, let alone Sadr City. It was ridiculous for anybody to think you could put a guy in a leadership role before he knew the job.

B-Town was instrumental in helping me navigate through and around the fragile egos. The former Marine said that he was fine with it, and he actually agreed with me. The two SEALs went along grudgingly only because they knew B-Town would kick their asses if they did not. One of the SEALs had shown up with a full-grown "Johnny Taliban" beard. When I told him that he would have to shave it or go home, he gave me some shit. He even went as far as asking me if the ambassador knew that beards were revered in Arab culture. He stated that all the DEVGRU guys had them. I explained that we were not kicking in doors and we were not trying to blend in with the locals, we were protecting "The Man." Beards were not acceptable. B-Town told him I was serious as a heart attack and if it was not gone the next morning that I already had a seat on a plane home for him. It was gone the next morning.

My replacement? Yeah, not so fine with the circumstances. Several times he tried to insist I introduce him to the ambassador as my replacement. When he finally realized I was not going anywhere, he then decided he wanted to be the shift leader. He tried to lobby the guys to his side. He called Blackwater. God only knows who else he tried to get help from. In all actuality

he was a good guy with a very solid background. If the circumstances had been different, he might have done a good job. He
had been misled by Blackwater, not by any of us on the detail. It
was just a very bad situation for all of us to be in. Unfortunately,
he was becoming a distraction and a morale killer to the team.
Mongo, the shift leader at the time, volunteered to step aside if
it would make my life easier. I told him: "No. Fuck no! That ain't
never going to happen." He remained the shift leader. End of
discussion.

Blackwater called me to try and press me to replace Mongo.
They went as far as to question his ability to do the job. I pointed
out that he had been in-country with us and The Dirty 30 for
months and had been on Karzai's detail in Afghanistan. He'd
also been the shift leader for almost three weeks at this point
and had done an excellent job. He knew the job inside and out.
There was no way I was going to weaken the team by putting an
inexperienced guy in a position to make the tactical decisions
before he knew the lay of the land. There was too much at stake
to take chances. I refused to budge. Blackwater was not getting
the intel reports I was getting every day, and, quite honestly,
they had zero idea what was going on. Why they thought they
knew more than the guys on the ground was a mystery to me
then and remains one even today. They did not know what they
did not know.

13 DECEMBER 2003

Brian Mac called me about 0200 and told me the boss needed to get to the office ASAP. I called Mongo. We got the guys up, headed over to the villa, picked Bremer up and brought him back. The ambassador went straight to his office to use his secure phone line. Brian came out and told me that there would be a press conference later that day at the convention center. At the press conference the ambassador announced that U.S. forces had captured Saddam. It was a great day for the coalition and the Iraqi people.

We got back to the palace and Brian came out saying we need to get to LZ Washington immediately. I asked where, and he said the airport. I told Brian I had no assets available for a proper advance and would need thirty minutes to prep. He said not to worry about it as the army would be picking us up. I grabbed the first four guys I saw, and we went to the LZ. We flew to BIAP in Blackhawk helos, got picked up by the military, and were quickly driven by U.S. military Humvees about ten minutes to Camp Cropper (a holding facility for "high value" security detainees). There were quite a few of the highest-ranking Iraqi diplomats standing there waiting for us, and I thought things are going to get interesting. And they did . . . very interesting.

We drove to a nondescript building being guarded by MPs. The ambassador and other diplomats went in. I trailed a few steps behind. I told my guys to stay outside. We walked down a hallway, and I could see what appeared to be cells. We walked into one, and there was Saddam. Not six feet away from me. He had been cleaned up, shaved, and was wearing the typical white Arab man dress with sandals on his feet. The Iraqis and Saddam seemed to be exchanging unpleasantries in Arabic, which I did not understand, but it was very stirring to be this close to the man who was a big part of the reason why I was in Iraq in the first place. Ambassador Bremer stood there, not saying a word, while the new leaders of Iraq confronted the former dictator. Saddam was quite full of himself and seemed angry that men he considered of lower status were even speaking with him. I went outside and let the other three guys, one at a time, take my place so they too could take a look at the tyrant. We were beyond excited.

Celebratory gunfire that evening rivaled any Fourth of July celebration. It felt as if we were under attack as tracer rounds and AK-47 fire filled the air. Fortunately, none of us were hit by the gunfire. None of the guys spent much time outside that evening, but when they did, they were hauling ass to their destination.

The ambassador was going to take a well-deserved break over Christmas and asked me if I wanted to go home for a few days. I immediately said yes. The guys would get a few days off to relax, and I would get to see the wife and kids. Win-win all around.

We had another rotation of guys planned for the following week. Sax, Ski, Doc Jones, Tony T, JD, the Chief, and a couple of the other remaining original guys were going to take off. Fortunately, so was the lead pilot. I was quite pleased because Hacksaw would now take over that job. With the original lead pilot departing, the big boy rules were now in full effect for all aspects of the detail. The pilots and ground crew could now actually sit down and eat chow with us and talk to us at the gym. Lines were no longer drawn between ground and air. Hacksaw allowed the ground and air guys to bond into a more combat-effective and cohesive team. After Hacksaw took the helm, he instituted joint weapons training, joint route recon planning, and the final standard operating procedures (SOPs) that we used for the duration of the mission. The days of the lead pilot whining about everything had finally ended. I will never understand why that guy could never get with the program. He wanted to make sure there was a clear division between the pilots and the ground guys—but why? Hacksaw, on the other hand, made sure that we were one team, and I knew he would sacrifice everything to make sure we did not fail in any way, shape, or form. He knew that keeping Ambassador Bremer alive was our sole overriding priority. I was ecstatic.

Hacksaw and Carl Magee (another Night Stalker vet) began calling the pilots and aircrews "the Ass Monkeys." Hacksaw even came up with a sign that proudly declared: WELCOME TO CAMP ASS MONKEY. This sign was posted at the entrance to the pilots' trailers at LZ Washington. Printed beneath the first line it said, "Fuck you. We have enough friends." It became our mantra. We found it hysterical.

Then, fortunately for me and my dwindling sanity, Ken rotated back in after a thirty-day home leave. I was extremely pleased. I now had one less headache to worry about. With Ken back handling the Ops/support, I no longer had to even think about it.

Doc Jones, a former Special Forces medic, took no shit from anybody. He was a gifted medic who constantly warned the married guys about PCOD (pussy cutoff date). Sexually transmitted diseases were not something you wanted to take home to your wife or girlfriend if you could avoid it. Doc gave his speech about every two weeks, warning married guys and those with significant others that they should refrain from intimate relations for a minimum of five days prior to returning home. This would give him a chance to "cure" the problem. He was a very funny guy, a team player willing to do anything to support his guys. During his stint he managed to "acquire" a ton of medical supplies from his Special Forces connections to treat our guys who got hurt or sick. Just before he rotated out he had had enough of my designated replacement's nonsense, and he offered to head outside with him and permanently shut his mouth. Fortunately, others in the office prevented a potentially ugly altercation.

Jadicus arrived right around this time and took over as my lead medic. We were supposed to always have two, but Jadicus was the main man and alone for several weeks. He had been a navy SEAL medic and was a stud. He was also one of the funniest guys on the team. Nothing and no one escaped his wit and sarcasm. He was very self-deprecating, and as often as he targeted someone else he also targeted himself. Having grown up with his Libyan family in Texas, Jadicus spoke fluent Arabic; and being a former frogman, he called himself "The Amphibian Libyan." He became my undercover eavesdropper. I would ask him to listen in on the conversations that the Iraqis were having around us, and to not let them know that he spoke the language.

It worked like a charm. He would report to us what the locals were saying. Sometimes it was good. Sometimes it was not so good. Jadicus never rotated out, and I was damn glad. Once he arrived he stayed with us until the ambassador left. He was a great asset and friend to me.

Jadicus also had the distinction of being the man who watched the Iraqi barbers when they came to cut the ambassador's hair. Jad would meet them at the barbershop, remove their razors and anything else that could potentially be used to kill Bremer, then graphically explain in Arabic how he hoped they would do something stupid so he could kill them. In their own language it made the threats even more real. Jad stared at these barbers as they worked, one hand on his Glock. He said nothing, but his look and demeanor said everything. The barbers always did an excellent job.

We made a trip down to Nasiriyah, a town about 230 miles southeast of Baghdad. I had sent four advance guys down the night before in the Little Birds so they could arrange security for the trip. It was going to be a quick in and out thing. The ambassador would be speaking at a town-hall-type event. We arrived at the LZ via Blackhawk, and one of B-Town's guys met us. The drive to the location took ten minutes. When we arrived, we saw a huge crowd milling about outside and coalition military forces attempting to establish control.

B-Town was inside the gate using his ASP baton to beat the fingers of the Iraqis who were attempting to scale the fence and get inside. He looked at me and just shook his head. This had all the warning signs of a bad day. We had already reduced the size of the detail team to accommodate "extra" members of the press on the security-designated Blackhawk. Apparently someone had given out more press passes than was the norm. To accommodate all the members of the press I was asked to take *all* security guys off the helo. I refused, but I did give up two seats. We got the ambassador inside and saw that the dais had been set up at the far end of the hall. We would have to walk through the crowd to enter and depart. Again I looked at B-Town. He quietly explained that this was not how he had told the organizers to set it up the day before. Now we were in it, and we would have to play it out as best we could. None of us was comfortable.

The crowd was mostly former Saddam military officers who had lost their jobs when Ambassador Bremer ordered Saddam's military disbanded. They were not a happy bunch. At one point a man stood up to speak and asked all the women in the room to leave. This was not good. Another guy stood up and began to sing.

Jadicus was listening to the Arabic when I radioed him and asked him what was going on. He said the audience was getting restless. So were we. I only had four advance guys and six detail members due to the limited seats on the helos. As the ambassador left the dais people started reaching for him. We formed a scrumlike formation around him and fought our way down along one wall. Our body armor and stout presence made it very difficult and impossible for them to reach through us and grab the ambassador. We finally made it out. It was the last time I ever gave up security seats on the helos to the press.

* * *

The day before I was heading home, I asked B-Town to take control of the team while I was gone, and he grudgingly agreed he would try. Welcome to my world I told him. I also instructed him to fire another misfit Ops/support guy who had somehow arrived in-country. It seems that Ken's replacement had somehow vouched for a good friend to come over and become part of the rotation. He knew that Ken did 99 percent of the work and his friend could just sit back and collect a check. B-Town just smiled and said he could handle it.

Brian B had come to Baghdad from Blackwater headquarters in Moyock, North Carolina, and I spent some quality time with him before I left. We discussed what was happening in Moyock and what was happening in Baghdad. We both agreed there was a huge disconnect between ground truth reality and what was being reported in North Carolina. He had a meeting with the ambassador where Bremer gave us high marks. Brian addressed the team and reiterated that I was staying and the issue between me and the program manager was just another case of two hard-headed Marines butting heads. The guys were happy and so was I. Truth be told, I half expected he was coming over to fire me.

On the day we left, our motorcade arrived at BIAP and there were eighteen wrestlers from the WWE waiting in the VIP lounge for the same C-17 to transport them back to the United States. They had been there doing a USO show for the troops. Stone Cold Steve Austin, the Big Show, and all the wrestlers were extremely good guys. They asked us to pose for pictures with them. It was pretty funny seeing these guys treating *us* like celebrities. When we landed in Germany, we boarded a small jet back to Andrews Air Force base. As Bremer and I left, I saw the guys from my team and the wrestlers at an airport bar. It was clear a good time would be had by all while they waited for their transport back to the United States.

We flew to the States on the small jet. I tried to sleep, but I was worried about what was happening with the guys back in Iraq. I was anxious to see Kim and the kids, and to be "normal" for a few days, but there was a nagging worry that the guys, without a focused job to do, might cause issues.

Back in the sandbox, B-Town quickly learned that sheep-dogging forty-six guys was no easy task. One of the new SEALs got drunk and destroyed the office. He was fired. Another SEAL missed a training mission with the Little Birds. He was given a verbal warning. A third former SEAL picked up a lady, headed over to the villa in the limo to show off, and managed to have a negligent discharge. (His M-4 rifle, not his dick.) This was kept from me until after he left. He never returned. All this in five days. Of course compounding the issue for B-Town were the other "leadership elements" who had arrived with him. While they were trying to undermine me in my absence, they were also gunning for him. Apparently the program manager (PM) back in North Carolina was severely ass hurt that his plans and promises to "his" guys had not borne fruit. It became quite real, about this time, that there were Frank-guys and the PM's guys. Unfortunately for B-Town, he was pegged as a Frank-guy. The reality was that B-Town had experience in the theater, the PM did not; B-Town knew what kept our guys and the ambassador alive, the PM did not. Fun times. B-Town was counting the days till I returned.

When I landed Kim met me at LGA and we went home. Being home was strange, very strange. No rocket or mortar fire. No helos flying overhead. It was scary quiet. I saw my mother, my brother Jim and his wife, Jen, and my niece Emma. And I got to spend some quality time with my daughters, Kelli and Katherine. Knowing that I was heading back and had no firm return date made it tough to relax. Kim was happy to see me, but I was not the same person. My innards twisted, and I constantly worried about what was happening to my guys. Kim tried hard, but I was still mentally trapped in Baghdad. I never could relax. It could have, and should have, been better than it was. I was unable to put Iraq on the back burner. It occupied my thought process at all times. Blackwater called and we talked for about two hours about many things. I felt that the air had been cleared. I was wrong.

The break ended abruptly. World events are tough to control. A massive truck bomb exploded at the gate into the Green Zone that we called "Baby Assassin's Gate." Brian Mac phoned, told me to get my ass back to D.C. ASAP.

We returned to the sandbox on New Year's Eve. The ambassador went to his villa; I returned to the madness. There were parties everywhere. I headed over to Blackwater Boulevard to see the guys and was met with a hero's welcome. It felt good to be back. Adult beverages flowed like water, and even the "new leadership" guys were partaking. It was weird to me and some of the others that they were partying hard with the same guys they had been reporting back to Blackwater for disobeying the rules. Two of them even managed to find female companionship. Truly a strange change of attitude. I guess, after they had been there a couple of weeks, they had decided my way of doing things was okay. Funny how it works sometimes.

A few days into January my "replacement" left, and a massive distraction to the team disappeared. No one mourned his departure.

A few new guys had arrived while I was gone. One of them was John "Cowboy" Hall. Cowboy had been a Marine drill instructor at Parris Island, then a cop in Texas. He was a big guy, gruff, and took no shit from anybody. While I was gone B-Town had placed him at the villa and had told him I would meet with him when I returned. Cowboy and I got together and he told me that given a choice he would like to be a door gunner on the Little Birds. I was fine with that, but knowing his USMC background I upped the ante and told him he could do it if he would run both the villa team and the door gunner team. Cowboy said, "Yeah. Hell, yeah." That day he became my first door gunner team leader. He was pleased and so was I.

As I mentioned earlier there had been a few occasions when guys failed to show up for training missions or were late to support a mission with the ambassador. Cowboy quickly rounded up Mid Day, Carmine, Nsync, Mike "Junkyard" Adamson, and Dave "Rooster" Bradfield to form the nucleus of a semipermanent door gunner team. Staffing of the detail was still hit or miss, but I knew with Cowboy at the helm the training missions would take place and the guys would show up on time. Hacksaw was pleased, the door gunners were happy, and it was one less headache for me.

JANUARY 2004

Sue Shea, Ambassador Bremer's personal assistant, had worked with him for years, including during his tenure at the State Department. She was a great lady and a true friend. Sue always looked out for the ambassador's best interests, and constantly gave me the heads-up about the crazy places and the impossible meetings other groups tried to have the ambassador attend. Some of the visits were extremely ill-conceived, others downright dangerous. Whenever she came to me with their harebrained ideas, I would reach out to my intelligence sources and try to get the real scoop on those places and areas. I knew full well if I approached the ambassador with the suggestion of cancelling a meeting, I had better have my ducks lined up in a way that supported and strengthened my case. There was no way I could simply tell the ambassador I thought this or that appointment was a bad idea without facts to back up my statements. He would have laughed me straight out of his office, and out of the country.

Sue also had a collection of nicknames for the people who worked there, and whom she had found to be less than honorable.

Suffice to say some of these nicknames were not fit for public consumption. I laughed like hell every time she would call me and say something to the effect of: "The dickhead from governance is trying to get you all killed again" or "Frank, Shit-for-Brains is at it again. You won't believe this one."

Sue took zero nonsense from anyone. She knew her job and did it exceedingly well. She was also not afraid to tell Ambassador Bremer exactly what was on her mind. One day, we took the ambassador to the office at 0630 as usual. He ate his breakfast at his desk and worked while he ate. Sue usually arrived at 0730. This particular morning she was making coffee when the ambassador popped out from his office and asked her, "Sue, I need the file on such and such."

Sue glared at him and said, "Damn it, Jerry, I just got here, you'll just have to wait a few minutes."

Q was on duty at the office door, and the ambassador looked at Q and said: "I guess she told me."

Q responded, "Yes, Sir. She did." All three of them then started laughing. That was Sue.

When Sue called, it was always business first and then it would get funny. So when a call came from her I knew it was serious. My phone rang one day and she said: "Quick Draw McGraw is making everyone in the office nervous."

I had no idea what she was talking about. I headed over there as quickly as possible. Sue and I retreated outside to have a cigarette while she explained to me one of my guys had been practicing his quick-draw techniques from his holster while standing office watch. I was not happy. Especially when she told me who "Quick Draw" was. Apparently, one of the "leadership" SEALs (yes, the one who had wised up and shaved his beard) who had arrived a few weeks before had decided that he should sharpen his quick-draw pistol skills while in an office filled with the ambassador's staff. This staff included the British ambassador, two full bird colonels, and about fifteen others. This was not good . . . especially with a loaded weapon.

I called B-Town and asked him to "talk" to his brother SEAL. B-Town by now was getting tired of dealing with these problems. He had a conversation with the guy that they kept between them. The antics stopped. At least in the ambassador's office.

A week or so later we took the ambassador to a meeting at the Al Rasheed where all the heavy hitters from the coalition forces were getting together. The advance team had set up the standard concentric rings of security; and in a huge change for me, I allowed the other PSD teams to carry their weapons inside. My thought process had been that all the high-ranking attendees were making us a huge target, and that the more guys we had with guns who could fight if there were a problem, the better it would be for all of us.

It was a huge PSD convention as well. Other U.S. teams, and many foreign teams, were there. We would be evaluated by all the others who desperately wanted to be us. Many had heard of Blackwater but had never met us. The hairy eyeball stares eventually stopped. We enjoyed each other's company and got to know them while they got to know us. There were probably one hundred or so guys milling about drinking coffee, telling stories, smoking and joking.

The sound an M-4 magazine makes when hitting a tiled floor, not to mention the sound of the ammo skittering across the floor, is unmistakable. Instinctively I smiled and turned around to see which idiot had dropped his magazine. Lo and behold, it was one of my guys. I contemplated suicide right there on the spot. The other PSD teams were laughing so hard that some of them were almost crying. And, you guessed it, it was "Quick Draw" again. I called B-Town on the radio and asked for a minute of his time. With an audible sigh he reported that he would meet me in two minutes.

"B-Town, WTF is the deal with your brother?"

"Father Frank, I know, I'll talk to him."

"Really, this shit has got to stop."

"Frank, how do you think I feel? He's an embarrassment to the Team guys."

"Well, I'm going to have to get rid of him."

"Please do. I can't take any more calls from you. You're killing me."

A week or so later, Quick Draw was gone. Not fired, moved to a different contract. Oh well, I warned them.

I had my first near miss with the Little Birds and door gunners around this time. For months Blackwater had failed to provide helmets and eye protection for our door gunners—let alone night-vision equipment. The guys had been flying wearing ball caps, watch hats, and sunglasses. The day after the full helmets arrived Cowboy was flying a day mission as a door gunner when a flock of feathered birds flew into his helo. Hacksaw got whacked in the face, and it nearly knocked him out. Cowboy took one directly in the visor. The helmet had saved his vision. Without the visor he definitely would have been blinded. He had about two dozen bird bones and feathers stuck in his face. Jadicus told him he looked like his face had been stomped by golf shoes. Jad cleaned him up, and Cowboy went back to work that afternoon. It was a miracle that Hacksaw had not lost complete control of the Little Bird and crashed. Cowboy was lucky that he had not been blinded. Lady Luck was still rooting for us.

We did finally get night vision goggles for the door gunners. Prior to that, only one shooter on each night mission had one. It was kind of funny that we had shooters who would not have been able to see what they were shooting at if there had been a problem. It was even more ironic because of the amount of shit I got from the air side about not providing dedicated door gunners from day one. We had an infrared beacon on the limo so that the pilots and the one door gunner with NVGs always knew where the boss was, but the other three shooters were, literally, in the dark. The cold was also an issue. Cowboy would wear four layers of clothes to keep warm while flying for hours at a time. He would even duct tape the opening of his clothes in an attempt to keep the cold air out. He looked like the Michelin Man from the tire commercials, but he was warm. Eventually, the others followed his lead. Fuck fashion, this was combat.

Blackwater at this time was going full throttle trying to win other Iraqi protection contracts. Based on the model we had developed and our solid track record, Blackwater had the inside track on most of them. Eventually, they did win several more contracts, and the Blackwater presence swelled from seventy-six (our detail of forty-six and the guys of The Dirty 30) to several hundred. Just like in the run-up to our detail, vetting and training was hurried, and some guys slipped through the cracks. I was happy that some of the Blackwater HQ attention had shifted from us to the numerous start-ups. Unfortunately, every time someone working for a new Blackwater team did something stupid, it landed in my lap. I spent many hours explaining that "we" only covered Bremer, not the rest of the country.

Many of my best guys, instead of coming back to me, were now being shuffled out to other programs. It seemed that the more I requested a particular individual, the less likely it was that I would get him back. And then a few of the other companies began to offer my guys considerably more money than Blackwater was paying, and I lost several others. Through all this shuffling the ambassador concentrated on nothing but rebuilding the country.

A typical day would go something like this:

0530: Muster in front of the palace in preparation for pickup

0545: Establish a security perimeter around the villa watching to see if anyone was watching us

0630: Take the boss to the palace; begin office watch (two guys)

0645: Check the schedule for any changes made overnight; check and respond to e-mails from Blackwater, etc.

0700: Eat chow

0730: Return to trailer

0745: Check with the advance team to see if they had everything they needed for the day

0800: Meet with the intel guys

0830: Digest the intel and check it against the schedule

0830: Advance team departs

0845: Meet with Sue to see what events were being planned

0900: Stage the motorcade for the first mission

0930: Head to the first event

1100: Return to the palace

1130: Eat chow

1145: Advance team departs

1215: Stage motorcade for the next mission

1245: Head to next venue

1400: Return to the palace

1415: Check schedule to see what changes have been made; notify advance team

1445: Advance team departs

1500: Stage motorcade

1530: Depart for next venue

1700: Return to palace

1715: Check schedule for changes, notify advance team if there are any

1730: Eat chow

1830: Check with the ambassador for a tentative departure time

2000: Stage motorcade for departure

2200: Depart for villa

2230: Return to palace

2245: Check schedule for changes for the next day; notify advance team if necessary; check for e-mails from Blackwater

2330: Return to trailer and sleep

This was a typical day. We longed for a time when the ambassador would work the entire day in his office, but at this point that was not happening.

The new gym finally opened, and we spent as much time there as we could in between runs around Baghdad. Most of the guys were gym rats of the highest order. And most were in great shape, and stronger than most other humans could ever dream of being. People would head over and see fifteen or twenty Blackwater guys in there, and they would just turn around and go back to their trailers. We probably had twenty guys who could bench well over three hundred pounds. At the pull-up bars our guys would wrap weights around their waists and see who could do the most reps. The dip bars became a place where guys contested who was strongest. It was like being around a professional sports team. Their bodies were their lifeblood; they counted on their strength and agility to save them, and they took their workouts very seriously. Ball busting was an everyday occurrence. Only the strong could survive.

We would monopolize all the forty-five-pound plates and most of the benches. If there were any women in there, the shirts quickly came off, and the scene was straight from muscle beach. The women loved being there. Other men hated us. Jealousy can be a bitch. We made more money than they did, had way cooler jobs than they did, and were in way better shape. It was a great way for us to blow off steam in a nondestructive manner. I encouraged the guys to spend as much time there as they could; and they did, if and when the schedule permitted.

The schedule was always a work in progress. The ambassador had to respond to every crisis that arose, and by this time they were coming fast and furious. The pressures that he dealt with every day would have crippled most people. He rarely, if ever got angry. He was an inspiration to the team. If he could do it at his age—sixty-two at the time—then we could hang in and support him. The guys truly admired him and his work ethic.

Rocket and mortar attacks against the Green Zone were now becoming a weekly event. Sometimes it was several times a week. Barrages usually consisted of about four rounds of incoming. We would hear the launch, then the explosion. It got to the point where we would do a quick check of our extremities, then move on or roll over and go back to sleep. Engineers installed a warning system on the palace grounds that garnered the moniker, "the Giant Voice." The massive loudspeakers advised everyone in the palace area of attacks—several minutes after they occurred. I'm sure that someone thought it was a great idea—maybe inspired by watching the old TV series $M^*A^*S^*H$. The explosions were very loud. Then the Giant Voice would advise us to take cover and remain there until the all clear was given. No shit, Sherlock!

The attacks never hit the trailer compounds—truly a miracle. The trailers would not have shielded us from much, as shrapnel would have opened them like cans of cheap dog food. Eventually a decision was made to put a series of sandbag walls around all the trailers to reinforce them. This meant that every day a legion of Iraqi workers arrived to fill and stack sandbags around the entire trailer park areas. The sandbags went around each and every trailer, and down the center of Blackwater Boulevard. The thought of these potential bad guys plotting and marking every inch of the living areas terrified us. With a simple GPS device they could have marked Blackwater Boulevard as a prime target. Whether they could hit it or not was another question. If they had, the injuries would have been a nightmare. They never did. Thank God.

Intelligence sources cautioned that I had become a stated target of the insurgents. Sax was also named. I guess the security measures we used pissed off the bad guys. They could not get close enough to even attempt to kill the ambassador. Sax and I laughed. Then the next report came in saying any Blackwater guy on the ambassador's detail was worth $50,000 U.S. dollars—dead. This was not funny. I called a meeting and told the guys that the stakes had been raised and to be even more vigilant as we did our jobs. We had zero injuries up to this point and I wanted to keep it that way.

One day, while attempting to sleep after an exhausting round of duty including a night shift at the villa and a day as a door gunner on the helos, Psycho was awakened from his slumber by the Iraqi day workers banging on his trailer—part of the ongoing sandbagging project. He stormed outside in his leopard-skin briefs with his M-4 at the ready and yelled at them: "Why can't you behave like a subjugated people?"

We laughed like hell. First because none of them spoke English, and second, because half my guys did not know what subjugated meant either. But an angry man in his underwear making threatening noises and carrying a rifle did make an impression on the workers. They stopped banging on his trailer.

The first week of January also witnessed the departure of my second set of drivers. The first group—Gino N, a former Marine and cop, had actually quit law school to take the job; JD, a retired SEAL; and WW, a former cop—had done a good job, but they were nowhere near the caliber of my second group: Q, Travis T, and FB. Q and FB had been driving instructors at BSR. BSR at that time was a world-class driver training facility and school located in Virginia. Most federal agencies used the facility to train their security drivers. These guys brought an air of professionalism that was unparalleled. From day one the ambassador felt much more comfortable when he saw Q behind the wheel. These guys had the skills that allowed us to travel faster and far more safely than with the original crew. Many guys can drive fast when they do not have to worry about other vehicles that are following them, or when they do not have the most-threatened man in the world in the backseat. Driving these fully armored, level-6 Suburbans that weighed around ten thousand pounds in tight formations, at high speeds, over obstacle courses while anticipating being shot or blown up, and making it look as effortless as if they were driving Volkswagen Beetles, was an amazing feat. I'm not going to say that they were the only guys who could have kept us alive during the assassination attempt, but I will say that I know the main reason we survived was due in large part to their unique skills. I was very sorry to see them leave. The next morning when we returned to the office the ambassador asked me where "his" BSR guys were. When I told him that had rotated out, he was not happy.

The morning that Q and his team departed, we ate breakfast in the chow hall around 0730. A guy came up to me and asked if he could speak to Q. As Q was sitting right there, actually right next to me, I found it comical. I told him that he had left the week before and asked what he wanted to talk to him about. Q glared at him and said nothing. The guy was wondering if Q could teach a driving class to his drivers. He claimed that Q had taught him a few years earlier while Q was working for BSR. Q is about six feet, five inches tall, weighs around 260 pounds, and is impossible to forget if you have ever really met him. We just shook our heads and smiled. The guy was working for a different company and knew his drivers were nothing compared to mine and were a liability to his protectees. I told him that I would mention it to Q, but that we were way too busy to be teaching others who did not work for Blackwater. Q laughed like hell. We never did do the training.

For about a week I could see by the look on the boss's face that he was not happy with Q's replacement. Larry, quickly dubbed Larrycade by the lead and follow drivers, was a decent driver, but he was much more cautious and deliberate in how he operated the vehicle. And slower. He simply did not have the skill level or the confidence that Q had. The limo sets the pace for the motorcade. I was constantly telling the other drivers to slow down so we could catch up. Scott S, another former BSR guy and former cop, and Dorian A, a former Marine, were going crazy trying to get Larry to maintain a greater pace. Speed meant safety. I began counting the days until Q returned. Only twenty-nine were left. I hoped. And I prayed.

As I mentioned earlier, 85 percent of all attacks happen in or around the vehicles. Handling those vehicles in an attack is a crucial skill set that few people understand. With Q gone, it became a constant source of concern to me. All three times we were attacked, it happened during motorcade operations. Enough said.

During a motorcade movement the tactical commander (TC) would call out potential threats to the limo as we moved down the road. The lead and follow cars responded by positioning themselves as a barrier between the limo and the threat.

TC: "Merging traffic right."

The lead would slow down while the follow car sped up, and the limo moved to the left alongside the lead and follow with the lead and follow between the potential threat and the limo. It was a form of ballet at 60 mph.

TC: "Parked car left."

Car bombs were a constant worry. We had to shield the limo from every parked car that we encountered.

TC: "Men with AKs on the right."

As I mentioned earlier, nearly every family in Iraq had an AK-47 in their houses. Crime was rampant, kidnappings for ransom were becoming commonplace, and the locals had to protect themselves and their families. We couldn't shoot at every person who was armed. We provided a blocking force between the potential threat and the ambassador. Even when they pointed guns at us, our rule was to cover the limo and get out of the kill zone.

On every mission, threats arose, yet we never engaged. We simply followed our basic training protocol—to keep the ambassador safe and get out of the kill zone as quickly as possible.

In mid-January there was an influx of people from the State Department. They had been sent over to begin turning the palace into the new U.S. embassy. They were a very serious bunch, and they knew how tough the job was going to be. As we were on a DOD contract I was technically not part of their support structure, but I also knew Blackwater was hoping to continue to do the security for the new ambassador who would be replacing Ambassador Bremer when and if he left. I gave them access to almost everything they asked for. I allowed them to use the helos to do a series of flyovers so they could get a sense of the Green Zone and its vulnerabilities. They needed to make additional security improvements to the villa with an eye toward housing a new ambassador. They were good people, and I was happy to help.

The ambassador had scheduled his trip to Davos, Switzerland, around this time. Davos was host to the World Economic Forum where the coalition partners were going to press the international community to donate money to help rebuild Iraq. It was a very important event. I told B-Town to pick some guys for the advance team and begin the preparations. Before Davos I would be flying back to the United States for a few days with the ambassador who was meeting with the president, then going on to New York to address the UN. B-Town would take the radios and other gear while I would carry the weapons with me and take them to Davos.

Jim Cawley from the Secret Service arranged for one of his guys to meet me at Andrews Air Force Base, and I gave him the weapons to hold until we departed in a couple of days. My guys were off to Switzerland. I gave them $10,000 in cash to cover their expenses and told them to be sure to get receipts. I talked to the advance team a few times while we were still in the States. They said everything was all set. A few days in Switzerland would be a welcome respite from Baghdad.

Unfortunately, real-world events intervened and the trip to Davos was canceled. We headed directly back to the sandbox. Once I got the word from Brian Mac that the boss was not going to Davos I contacted B-Town and advised him to try and get back to Baghdad as quickly as possible. It took them five days. When I asked for the receipts to square up the $64 in change they gave me, they quickly scribbled out some homemade, handwritten ones. Apparently it is quite expensive in Switzerland! We still laugh about it. B-Town, Jadicus, Mongo, and Swiss Mike must have had a good time. They had scouted out more than a few restaurants, ski areas, hotels, bars, and entertainment areas that the ambassador would be able to enjoy if he had been able to find the time. I often wonder if any of them would have been on the ambassador's short list of places to go.

Ken was back now, and somehow he fixed it. Getting the hotel and airlines to fax the receipts to him was not easy, but he was a pit bull when it came to the Ops/support stuff. He made sure we were looked after while we were taking care of the ambassador. We never had to think about the support efforts going on behind the scenes.

Intel reports were still gloomy, but we soldiered on. The pace continued at its incredible rate. One day the boss was at the Al Rasheed and scheduled to go from there to a meeting at the home of a leading Iraqi diplomat. The advance team headed to the man's house. While they were moving into an intersection, a group of individuals came out and began to fire at their convoy with AK-47s. Following proper procedures they drove out of the kill zone and no one was hurt. I made the decision to abort and told them the meeting was canceled and to return to the Green Zone. Then I told the ambassador there had been an attack on the advance team, and he would not be going. Once again he was relieved that none of us had been hurt.

When we returned to the office we found out that this leading Iraqi diplomat had not been in his house but had expected the meeting to take place in his office. Even paranoid people have enemies, and I wondered where the miscommunication had taken place. Our office would not have screwed that up; it had to have come from the Iraqi side. Throw in the attack and the whole thing stunk. We had been misled and led directly into an ambush. Not a good thing to dwell on, but it opened our eyes even wider.

About this time I earned my call sign. Everyone had some type of call sign that we used when talking over the radio. There were rules associated with call signs. Earning a call sign is like being knighted, but instead of a sword on the shoulder from the Queen, it was bestowed by the team. Guys did not pick their own; and you could not do anything about the one bestowed. They could be region based, sport based, ethnic based, or looks based. There was no telling what a group of type A smart-asses might come up with. And if you rebelled against it, it stuck even tighter. We had the guys who were part of the "Boy Band" a.k.a. Nsync. With an age range from mid-twenties to early fifties we covered the entire spectrum of conceivable names. And so it went—you got it, you lived with it. Up to this point, I had been just Frank, and I was fine with that.

Then the boss made a trip to Kurdistan, and I decided that I could use the two days to relax and recharge my batteries. The Peshmerga, the finest members of the Kurdistan military forces who oversaw security up there, were top-shelf guys. After a few trips up there, I realized that the ambassador was quite safe when visiting with the Talabanis or the Barzanis. These two families were the longtime leaders of the Kurdish people and had fought long and hard against Saddam for decades. I told him I would not be going and that Drew would be in charge. He confirmed he was fine with that.

Later that day, Erik Prince, the owner of Blackwater arrived in-country. He was not there for us, but to take a look at some of the other fledgling start-ups, and to look at other possible business opportunities. I was with about fifteen other Blackwater guys in the Green Zone Café, the first bar and restaurant to open up in the Green Zone. It very quickly became a popular spot for everyone working in the palace area. The food was fair, but the beer was cold. (Unfortunately, the café was blown up via a backpack bomb shortly after Bremer left the country.) Two liquor stores had also opened around this time, so our periodic runs for alcohol into downtown Baghdad or to the duty-free shop at BIAP ended. At least a few of the Iraqis had learned about capitalism, and supply and demand, and that the coalition folks would spend money if they could find what they wanted to buy.

After a few hours, the mountain of beer cans on the table reached epic proportions, and I warned the guys that we should clean them up just in case anybody walked in.

Scotty S was sitting next to me. He declared loudly: "Blackwater can kiss my white ass, I work for Frankwater!"

Cowboy John H quickly repeated the mantra: "Blackwater can kiss my white ass too, I work for Frankwater!"

The other maniacs roared in approval while I tried to click my heels together three times and wake up in Kansas. I had my radio with me but it was quickly snatched from me while Scotty S and Cowboy John H repeatedly called for Frankwater over the air. I made the colossal mistake of trying to explain why this was a really bad idea. And I got: "Fuck 'em. They always try to fuck us over, and you take care of us. We work for you. Fuck 'em!"

I sincerely hoped that Erik was not listening. But it was too late even if he wasn't. These guys had made a decision, and I was stuck with it. The calls to Frankwater quickly went viral, and all

I could do was ask for another beer. Eventually, they even made much-coveted Frankwater T-shirts.

The guys who made that trip to Kurdistan also had an interesting trip. They had flown into a snowstorm in the mountains and the Blackhawks had been in a whiteout situation. They had nearly flown into the side of a mountain on the way to the meeting. Lady Luck was still on our side.

Bill Miller, now firmly in control as the new regional security officer, knew that we did not have any automatic weapons. I had casually asked if there were any "squad automatic weapons" (SAWs—5.56-caliber fully automatic belt-fed machine guns) around that we could mount in the Little Birds to provide additional firepower in the event one of the intel reports proved to be correct. He promised to keep his ears open and keep me posted. Ken D came to me and said he had access to four SAWs that were being turned in by another government contractor who was leaving the area. I immediately said we wanted them. He told me he would check with Bill Miller, and if I was approved, and if I would sign for them, we could have them. A few hours later I signed for the four SAWs.

Hacksaw and I talked about how to best utilize the new weapons. He said he wanted them in the Little Birds, but *only* if he could put the door gunners through a training program. Of course I said yes. Cowboy, Carmine, Hacksaw, and Cat Daddy got together and figured out the best way to mount them, and we started the SAW door gunner program. As luck would have it we did not have enough ammo for the training program, and I had to whore out the helos again before we could become completely and safely operational. At the same time, my magician, Ken, was working some serious deals to get as much SAW ammo in their specific plastic boxes from "friends of the movement" that he could scrounge. He somehow acquired around two thousand rounds and had a line on more. When I asked where and how he got it, he smiled and said, "Don't ask . . . you don't want to know."

Ammo in hand, Hacksaw designed a comprehensive program that would enable the door gunners to provide and direct firepower on the designated targets, and not hit the motorcade or shoot down our own helos. It was at this point that my Little Bird education became much better rounded. For instance, Hacksaw explained to me that as the weather went from hot to hotter-than-hell, the lift capability of the helos was hindered. When Hacksaw had asked me to give him door gunners who weighed 180 pounds or less, I thought he had lost his mind. I had been sending guys over who were easily 200 pounds or more. It had never occurred to me that hot air had less density than cooler air, and therefore the helos had to work a lot harder to fly in it. DUH! I apologized, and he just laughed.

The difference between the semiautomatic Bushmaster M-4s Blackwater had provided and these fully automatic SAWs was daunting. If anybody made the mistake of attacking us, our response now would be much more lethal. And with this increase in lethal capability came an increase in potential liability. Hacksaw and I talked in length about why he would now need designated door gunners who would be at his disposal and available for training whenever possible. Fuck me. I knew he was right, but I was still juggling the number of guys I had to cover the villa, the advance team, the detail team, and office watch.

And then, just like in the movies, the skies opened up, the stars aligned, and Blackwater got the contract modification it had requested the previous September. The original contract had not included the security staffing at the villa. I got word that I had fourteen additional men inbound. Twelve were designated as villa only, and the other two were coming to me. A few days later I had a contingent of sixty. Hacksaw and I decided that he would need six guys to complement his operation. Four would fly, and two would be on standby if things got ugly. I asked him who he wanted, and he began reviewing the backgrounds of the guys he was considering. Some of the guys were pissed they were chosen, some were pissed they had not been chosen, and some were just pissed off all the time anyway. Just another day in the sandbox.

Hacksaw chose eight guys to try out and then kept the six he liked best. He was happy, Blackwater was happy, and I was happy that everybody else was happy. The training program was intense. Flying in the Little Birds with former TF-160 pilots for hours at a time is like being strapped to the hood of a Ferrari and driving around a road course at 200 mph. Air sickness was not uncommon. Hacksaw's only rule was if you barfed, you cleaned it up when you got back. And the ball busting was merciless.

In Hacksaw's previous life with TF-160 he had been the lead Little Bird pilot instructor and had devised the Little Bird training program and shooting courses that the spec-ops community still uses today. I could not ask for a better Little Bird mentor. He knew what worked and why it worked. And he could teach it. What a lot of people don't realize is the Little Birds are not armored helos. A round as small as a .22 could easily take one down. The margin for error in the Little Birds was extremely small, and we relied upon them as our first-line quick reaction force (QRF). If something happened, they would hover over the action and make life miserable for whomever was trying to kill us. Hacksaw knew this, and he pushed the door gunners to be perfect in everything that they did. He also had the unenviable task of training the new pilots who came in. Apparently finding qualified Little Bird drivers is not easy, and he often got guys who had never flown Little Birds. Some had been Blackhawk pilots, Apache pilots, Huey pilots, etc. Just because a guy had been a helo pilot did not mean that he could fly the high-performance sports cars that we were using in a combat zone. Hacksaw would give them no more than ten days to get to the level of performance that he demanded, or he would send them home. Many did not make it. Some just could not grasp the fundamentals, some could not fly with the night vision goggles, and some were just scared. We had one guy who arrived, took his first training flight, and experienced his first mortar attack on his day one. He quit on his day two. All within thirty-six hours. It took a special breed of pilot to do what these guys were doing—especially when the realization set in that the support system was just us. No one was on standby if one of the helos went down. They were on their own. The adventure and adrenaline rush quickly dissipated for more than a few. It was hard, scary work—a true test of intestinal fortitude.

The Bremer team surrounding the boss, December 2003.
Photo by Christina Estrada Teczar.

Departing Saddam's palace in Tikrit after meeting with high-ranking
coalition military leaders, April 2004. Photo by Christina Estrada Teczar.

Another photo from the Tikrit meeting, April 2004.
Photo by Christina Estrada Teczar.

Just another gentle reminder that the insurgents did not like the coalition folks. Smoke and debris immediately after a mortar and rocket attack in the Green Zone, March 2004. Photo by Travis Haley.

Saddam's pool early in the day before the lunch and evening crowds descended on it. Photo by Kristen Whiting.

One of the many signs that led to the entrance of Blackwater Boulevard, where the team lived. These logos showed up one morning after an evening of shenanigans. I have an idea who did it (Geek), but no one ever took credit. Photo by Christina Estrada Teczar.

Talking strategy: detail team leaders—me, Drew, and Riceman—and the tactical commander of Tikrit. Photo by Christina Estrada Teczar.

Heading back to the motorcade after a meeting with some of our European coalition partners. Photo by Christina Estrada Teczar.

Returning to Baghdad International Airport via USAF C-130 after a trip to Mosul. In typical war-zone fashion, the aircraft did not shut down for us to deplane. Photo by Christina Estrada Teczar.

With Nsync and Drew, taking the boss to another meeting, February 2004. Photo by Christina Estrada Teczar.

A three-vehicle motorcade departing the palace for another run into the Red Zone. These level-6 armored SUVs weighed nearly ten thousand pounds, making them hairy to drive in combat situations. Photo by Travis Haley.

Blackwater guys taking a break during a lull in the action on the roof of the Coalition Provisional Authority (CPA) headquarters in Najaf, April 2004. Photo by Travis Haley.

A Thursday-night pool party! The festivities were just beginning, May 2004. Photo by Kristen Whiting.

A Little Bird with Hacksaw and Cat Daddy behind the controls, taking off to keep the bad guys away, May 2004. Photo by Christina Estrada Teczar.

Arriving during a sandstorm via Little Bird for the reopening
ceremony of the Baghdad train station, May 2004.
Photo by Christina Estrada Teczar.

Returning to LZ Washington from a meeting in Tikrit.
Drew and HB manning the flank. Photo by Jason Howe.

Ambassador Bremer shaking hands with a Blackhawk crew member
after another successful mission. We completed several hundred
thousand "Blackhawk frequent flier miles" during our tenure there.
Photo by Jason Howe.

The last day of The Bremer Detail: the team relaxing on the
night Ambassador Bremer and I left the country, June 2004.
Photo by Christina Estrada Teczar.

FEBRUARY 2004

As the time approached for the assembled American and Iraqi diplomats to write a constitution for the new Iraq, a thousand different forces pulled Ambassador Bremer in a thousand different directions. We had several Red Zone missions every day, winding up with meetings at the Iraqi Governing Council (IGC) building until late each night. Exasperation began to show on all the diplomats as the divergent groups of Iraqis argued for all their pet projects, each attempting to sway every law and every decision to favor his own special interests. Each day we visited several different politicians before heading over to the IGC, and each evening we witnessed the politicians apparently forgetting the agreements they had made with the Americans earlier in the day.

My guys were dragging ass. The original villa guys rejoined the detail and advance teams after being replaced by the new, designated villa team and were being trained by the advance team leader and shift leaders on how to do their newly assigned jobs. It was like a sports draft where I allowed each team leader to make a selection to fill the holes left by the newly crowned door gunners. Each group had lost damn good guys to the helos. And they were pissed about their degraded operational capacities. Again, being in charge sucked. Hacksaw was happy, but the two guys I relied upon the most—the shift leader and the advance team leader—were pissed off. Some days you just could not win. I just put my head down and went back to work, convincing myself that one out of three really wasn't that bad. Hell, in baseball I might have made the Hall of Fame.

The selections were finalized, and the train-ups began. Eventually I got to the point where each group had enough bodies to have two squads. I made the decision at this point to split the detail team into two separate entities. Group 1 would work from 0530 to 1500, and Group 2 would replace them at 1500 and take the helm until we took the boss home. We would do a one-week rotation. This way each group got to sleep in every other week. Initially it sounded like a good plan. The problem was the Red Zone runs. My master plan soon evolved into a Red Zone team and a Green Zone team. There was no way I could, nor would I ever, skip a Red Zone move; and after a few Red Zone moves with teams that were not as sound as I felt they should be, I scrapped the original idea of rotations. So I designated a dedicated Red Zone group shortly thereafter. The Red Zone team was made up of my best guys. If we had no Red Zone moves planned, we would split the day.

I also made the decision the drivers were too valuable to rotate. Q and his guys had returned and I needed them to stay as sharp as possible while I was working their asses off. This meant some extremely long days. To try to even the field a bit I took them completely off office watch and told them to sleep whenever they could. When trapped at the IGC, I instructed them to sleep in their cars. I needed Q and his partners as fresh as possible. To operate at the level that Q and his crew did took massive concentration and unmatched skill. No one was running motorcade operations like us. No one. Q, Travis T, and FB created the tactics that are now in large part the SOP for PSD high-threat motorcade operations. When other PSD teams joined our motorcade on a Red Zone move, they could not keep up. They could not match the speed and the precision driving with even just two cars. We were still operating with three level-6 Suburbans plus our MP CAT teams, and it was truly poetry in motion as we moved around the city.

I took the advance team off office watch as well, as they were busting their asses planning and executing multiple security procedures at disparate sites and events. I needed them focused at all times. And with the operational tempo, we were often splitting the advance team up to leapfrog ahead of us as we visited the next venue. The advance guys always had to be there before us, and always stayed behind to cover our departures. It was a hectic time for them.

In the limo we had an electronic countermeasure (ECM) device designed to defeat radio waves, telephone signals, and anything else the bad guys used to remotely detonate IEDs. There was a way to program the thing to block only certain signals, but outside of Geek, none of us really knew how to do it. Geek was an electronics genius. He was also a former Air Force spec-ops guy who had been part of the team that had rescued Jessica Lynch, who had been captured early in the war and taken hostage. Our spec-ops guys conducted a successful rescue operation on an Iraqi hospital where she was being held. Oftentimes while traveling through bad areas we would turn the ECM on, but then lose our own radio and phone capabilities. The pilots would get pissed, as they would see things and not be able to relay the information to us. It was a great tool, but also one we had to use judiciously. The devices used in those days had a radius of about two hundred meters.

Of course, boys being boys, we also realized quickly we could have a bit of fun at other people's expense when they would try to use their cell phones. Cell-phone service in the Baghdad area sometimes was great, but sometimes extremely poor. Parking in front of the palace waiting for the ambassador to come out provided ample playtime for guys who had evil minds, strange senses of humor, and toys at their disposal. When there was nothing to keep them truly occupied, the idle time became the devil's time.

I would be in the office waiting for the signal from the ambassador that he was ready to move, and I would hear over the radio: "Stand by. Activate." Followed by howling laughter. Then, "Tell that moron to get off the phone and go back to work."

The guys had favorite targets they abused. Some had taken condescending attitudes toward us. Others had been hostile or made snide remarks about the "mercenaries." A few just rubbed the guys the wrong way. The guys heard the remarks and saw the sneers, but never retaliated. Not then anyway. In time they would get some payback. The usual sequence went like this:

We'd see someone come out, reach for his phone, start to dial, say hello, then we'd activate the ECM. A second or two later the target would realize he had no service. We'd then hear some expletive, and the guy would stare at the phone, look up into the sky, and walk in circles attempting to reclaim the signal. Deactivate. Signal returns. Dial, say hello . . . Activate! Lather, rinse, repeat. We found it hysterical. We would do it until the target went back to work. I know we were children, but it was funny. Especially when it happened over and over to certain people who spent more time trying to make a phone call than working in their offices. DOD had managed to get cell phones with New York area codes, and folks were dialing direct to the States. Many abused the privilege——to the tune of phone bills amounting to hundreds of thousands of dollars per month.

There is one rule that all life takers and leg breakers should know: Never let the other guys know when something truly bothers you, or you will have that scab picked off at every opportunity. Combine this with the strict set of rules that governs the complex skill of talking over the radio—only essential traffic, only one person talks at a time—and it sets up . . . well, you'll see.

By now we knew each other's voices and call signs like the back of our hands. Only my team had access to our radios, and our frequencies and our conversations were only monitored by us. The guys had really outrageous senses of humor, and when boredom set in there was no telling what might come across the airwaves. It was way better than Comedy Central. Not only did I not try to rein in it in, I joined in. It kept the guys loose, and it was a good way for morale to stay high.

So one night, after a series of twenty-hour days, I remained behind when the team went to the IGC building. I put my designated replacement, the so-called Marine "leadership" guy, in charge of the detail. Security at the IGC was extremely tight because all the important people in Iraq met there regularly, often at the same time. Brutus was back with us after stints with The Dirty 30—I was damn glad to have him—and this evening he was working with the advance team. Matt B, also known as 2-Ts, was there as well.

My designated replacement for the evening decided to take this opportunity to assert his leadership skills and to instill some sense of discipline into the guys. We had a bad habit of blowing into our radios when we got bored. We did it sometimes to see if our radios were working or just to get about a dozen other guys to repeat what we had done. It was harmless to the nth degree. 2-Ts blew into his mike, and Brutus responded in kind followed by half a dozen others. My replacement got on his radio and told the guys to stop the "unprofessional" behavior. This was followed by almost every member of the team blowing up the radio frequency with more of the same.

Mr. Leadership got pissed. "Okay, I've had it. The next guy that does that will get sent home. I'm telling Frank as soon as we get back."

Oh dear God. He could not have reacted in a worse fashion. The guys had a field day at his expense.

"I'm in charge. I'm ordering you to stop that right now."

More blowing ensued. My phone rang while I was trying to sleep. This guy is almost crying in frustration that the men have no respect for him. I explain that respect is earned, not given by nature of a title, and that some of the guys had been here long before him. It was not evident to any of them that he knew their jobs better than they did, or that he was more professional than they were. He said he wanted them all fired. I reminded him of the fact I also blow into the radio, and that by extrapolation he was accusing me of being unprofessional. I said, "We'll talk in the morning," and hung up. Needless to say, the unprofessional radio protocol continued all night.

The next day the guys came to me and described Mr. Leadership as a stress monster, saying they would never work under him again. He had destroyed any iota of credibility that he had built to this point. It only takes one bad day to fuck up your reputation in the shark tank. He fucked it up, not under attack but in the Green Zone. Not a good thing. He rotated out a few days later.

Guys rotating out and then back in create new issues. Each day we tweaked our tactics. The changes were seldom dramatic but they were cumulative. Being out of the loop for thirty or sixty days meant the SOPs had changed since a guy had last worked with the detail in the sandbox. What had worked during his last stint may have no longer applied due to intelligence we had received or the equipment we were now using. I was not trying to hurt anybody's feelings, but I would never replace an existing shift leader, advance team leader, or TC until he rotated out. The returning guys would just have to wait their turn. Most guys were mature about it, but some were babies of the highest order. Apparently the size of their dick was directly proportional to the size of their job. Sorry for your loss, but the ambassador's safety, and the safety of my team, always came first.

By this time Blackwater's presence in-country had grown rapidly and dramatically. Hundreds of guys were now working on multiple contracts throughout Iraq. There were guys that I wanted back—Shrek, Tony T, Dorian A, James C, and others—who were instead sent to other locations to do other jobs. Some, I was glad to lose. Others, I fought tooth and nail to keep. Nsync and G-Money came to me one day and said they were being sent to different gigs. I told them I wanted them to stay. They weren't sure what to do as they had been told they were going. I explained that the dangers in Iraq were getting worse each day and that to go to a start-up operation was foolish and dangerous. Besides, The Bremer Detail was Blackwater's identity: Did they really want to protect food convoys or work for lesser-ranking Coalition Provisional Authority (CPA) diplomats? I lobbied Blackwater on their behalf, and they stayed. I was pleased.

The first team leader at the villa, Sergeant Major P, was a former Army Ranger quite famous for his tenure as the lead instructor at the Army Ranger School. He had been highly decorated in Vietnam, had served over thirty years in the Rangers, had been on the Desert One rescue mission, and was in the Ranger Hall of Fame and one of the first and original members of Delta Force. He ran the villa like an infantry company. He would even have show-of-force drills where all his guys would march around the villa with all their gear, so if the bad guys were watching they could see what they were up against. His guys did not get much time off. He would even hop in a truck and do recon runs through the Red Zone to see what the locals were doing. The sergeant major was a good man, and he was hard. I knew I would never have to worry about the villa as long as he was there. He had spent his entire adult life in the army at the tip of the spear. He truly lived for the action.

✣   ✣   ✣

The hours at the IGC exhausted us. Ambassador Bremer averaged three hours of sleep each night, yet marched on. He was amazing. The meetings were brutal to witness. Talk, more talk, bargain, and then a thirty-minute break while each different group ran out to call someone and ask how they should vote. They were the future leaders, yet none of them could make a damn decision. The ambassador huddled with his staff, waited for the Iraqis to return, then they all rehashed the same ground. And the process would repeat—talk, bargain, retreat to call someone for instructions.

By this time my guys had the ECM device down to a science. The Iraqis were given exactly five minutes to talk; then mysteriously all cell phones would die. They would wander in circles for a few minutes hunting for a signal before heading back inside. The breaks became much shorter. We like to think that we had a hand in hastening the writing of the legal code. It almost bit us in the ass one evening, however, when they had called for a break and the ambassador was meeting with his staff. I heard the "Stand by. Activate." command and the laughter. Just then the ambassador turned to Brian and said, "Get Condoleezza (Rice) on the phone."

I almost died.

"Cease fire. Deactivate now," I barked. Fortunately the guys were able to kill it before it hampered the ambassador's call. I breathed deeply when Brian handed the ambassador the phone, and he said hello to the secretary of state.

— 173 —

Bagdad's electricity was supplied primarily by generator. The IGC building was no exception. One day the ambassador told me he wanted to see one of his Iraqi counterparts who had an office on the seventh floor. There was an elevator, but we were always hesitant to use it as power outages were quite common. I asked the ambassador if he wanted to walk the seven flights or take the elevator. The stairwells were not air-conditioned, nor were they clean. There were always mounds of trash that we would have to climb over. He opted to use the elevator. The elevator had enough room for me, Sax, and the boss. As we entered the cage I heard Drew tell some of his guys to form security on the ground floor and tell Jadicus and another man to head to the seventh floor. As the elevator doors opened on seven I saw Jadicus and G-Money standing there waiting for us stone-faced and playing it cool after sprinting up seven flights of stairs in 115-degree heat. The ambassador smiled at them knowing that they had busted their asses to beat him up there. They had their body armor on, weapons, radios, etc. As I escorted the ambassador to his meeting I caught Jadicus and G-Money out of the corner of my eye as they doubled over and tried to catch their breath. Their beating us up to the seventh floor wasn't a miracle—it was a testament to their level of fitness.

The pace continued unabated. Intelligence reports never got any better. The team was more relaxed now due to the increase in manpower. At least now, when a guy was sick or hurt, he had a chance to rest up before I dragged him kicking and screaming back into the fray. I even began to think that we would survive this thing.

The emotional burden of being in command of the detail defies description. On the one hand there was the mission. I would die before I let something happen to the ambassador. And I was going to do everything in my power to make sure that I cheated, lied, stole, cut every corner, and/or anything else that was necessary to make sure that none of my now sixty guys got hurt. About this time the insurgency elevated both the frequency and level of terror and violence throughout the country. Attacks against U.S. and coalition forces picked up. The attacks against the Green Zone continued. Convoys routinely hit IEDs or received incoming small-arms fire. The assaults affected our supply lines—especially for fuel. It became so bad that Q and his guys had to siphon gas from destroyed vehicles so that we could get the fuel we needed to get the ambassador to his appointments. How they sometimes got gas I will never know—and I don't think I want to.

I missed both Kelli's and Katherine's February birthdays. I talked to them frequently on the phone, and I always tried to sound happy and upbeat. Kim was doing the best she could to cope with my "thirty-day absence," which had now stretched to almost six months—with no end in sight. The stress beat on me. At the same time I would have guys come to me and unload about their issues at home and ask to get some time off. It was easy to nod and to say that I understood, but the mission came first. If I let one guy go, then others would ask. I had become a cyborg, a machine that was focused on doing what had to be done. There was no room for weakness. I had to lead from the front. By this time I had lost about twenty pounds. My clothes didn't fit. I had guys bring me stuff when they returned or had Kim mail me various items.

Much thanks to Colonel Sabol—when Bird rotated out, the colonel had allowed me to keep the trailer to myself. It was my sanctuary, my refuge, my alone place. I could punch and kick the walls, and no one would witness it. I was tired. I missed my kids. I needed a break. Still I did my best to keep the team loose and smiling and at the top of their game. It was tough.

A few good things happened this month. The weather got warmer, and a slew of new women arrived at the palace. Nurses, Air Force officers, State Department employees, and civilians. The ratio of men to women dropped to about 35 to 1. Nice. Prior to their arrival the palace pool had been a major sausage festival. Our European male counterparts would lounge out there in their Speedos and rub oil on each other. We would throw up in our mouths whenever we walked by. It was revolting. Now, however, the chance to spot women increased. At lunchtime we began sending a scouting party to the pool to see who was there and to give us a sitrep regarding the ladies. Watching these ladies rub oil on each other sure beat the hell out of watching the guys. And now, with the new rotation schedule, almost half my guys had the evenings off. Our attendance at the parties increased, and so too did the friendships we made with folks who had initially watched us from afar and had decided we were assholes because we had no time to meet and talk with them. People now said hello or waved rather than shaking their heads in disgust or avoiding us altogether. This was a great public relations coup for the team and for Blackwater.

Ayatollah Hussein al-Sadr was one of the leading Shiite clerics in Iraq. He was a good friend and confidant of the ambassador, and we made several visits to his home while we were there. He was also the uncle of Muqtada al-Sadr, the leading anti-American cleric in Iraq. The nephew constantly stirred up his followers and called for death to all Americans. At times he was successful. Trips from the palace to his uncle's house, usually for dinner, were stressful as hell. They meant taking a long ride, at night, through bad-guy country. The advance team, as always, got there before us and deployed their troops in an order to keep the ambassador as safe as possible.

Hussein al-Sadr had his own security team. As a sign of respect to us, they always let me into his house to see where the ambassador would be during the meeting or meal. And as a sign of respect to them, I always went in and came straight out. They did not have a security presence in the room, and I was damn sure not going to embarrass them by insisting that I stay inside. Their head of security was a nice man who spoke decent English and always provided us with water and fruit drinks. His men, however, kept a wary eye on my men at all times. It was pretty evident they did not like us or trust us. But truth be told, we felt the same way about them. I guess we were even.

One of our first visits there had been with Secretary of State Colin Powell. The Diplomatic Security (DS) agents had accompanied us. It was hot. They were in suits and ties, and they stuck out like sore thumbs. After about two hours, one overweight agent, suffering from the heat, dropped his rifle into the raw sewage that was running down the gutter next to where the motorcades were parked. We laughed about it every time we returned. Al-Sadr's head man always made a point to ask me if I was really sure that that it had not been one of my guys. It was our inside joke. Another time he pulled me aside and said that he had just received word that "people" were waiting for us on our departure. He hugged me and said, "God be with you." He then turned and went directly inside before I could ask any questions.

He had never done that before. Was it a cryptic warning of an attack he had heard about? I wanted to rush after him, but the meeting was breaking up and the ambassador was saying his good-byes. We had three minutes to change up our plan.

I grabbed the shift leader and the TC and told them to figure out a route we had never taken before and to brief the Little Bird pilots, the CAT MP commander, and the advance team leader. They did, and we got home without incident. Another evening at Hussein al-Sadr's home we noted new guys on his security team. I always had an Arabic speaker, usually Jadicus, with us. He never spoke Arabic in the presence of Iraqis. I wanted them to speak freely while thinking that the stupid Americans could not understand them. This particular night we got an earful from these new guys.

"These Americans think they are so tough. We could kill them easily. They think they can fight, we'll show them how to fight. If I point my rifle at them, I bet they would piss their pants." And so it went. We just smiled and secretly prayed and hoped that they would do something stupid. They never did. Thank God.

On another one of our Hussein al-Sadr visits we were attacked on the way home. The detail had departed with the ambassador, and the advance team followed a few minutes behind. The advance team was the first on-site to make sure it was safe for us, and they stayed behind to make sure we got the ambassador into the motorcade and were on our way before they departed. Our advance team ran a motorcade identical to the detail team—three black Suburbans and an MP CAT team. The only difference was the advanced team had an additional vehicle with the dogs. This night, as the advance team approached an intersection a man stepped into the street and tossed a bomb under the middle vehicle. The bomb went off, but thanks to poor timing it exploded between cars, not beneath one. Still, the front tires were shredded. The team did not stop and engage, but quickly *Got off the "X"!* That is, we outran the kill zone. Thank God our vehicles were equipped with run flats. Run-flat tires have a solid core so that in the event they go flat, you can still drive on the solid core. Not very comfortable, but they allowed us to get off the "X" and keep moving. All our men made it home. Brutus called me afterward to tell me that I had promised him he would not be killed on this gig. I told him that I might have lied, but that I hadn't lied yet.

MARCH 2004

On 8 March, the U.S. delegation and the Iraqi Governing Council finally finished and signed the county's new administrative law. We were quite pleased. Unfortunately the overall Iraqi population was not. The rate of attack against coalition assets accelerated. Convoys were routinely destroyed. Coalition hostages were being taken and beheaded as the Shia took out decades of grievance on the Sunni, and the Sunni responded in a tit-for-tat cycle of revenge for revenge's sake. The tension became palpable. Ambassador Bremer drove on as though he had just arrived. We had fuel shortages, food shortages; the BIAP road became a shooting gallery. Each mission felt more dangerous than the previous one.

As the roads got worse the CPA folks tried to move food from BIAP to LZ Washington via helicopter, but that couldn't keep up with demand due to the number of people now at the CPA. The chow hall began to ration food—one scoop per person. We lived on really bad grilled cheese sandwiches, really bad chicken nuggets, and hard-boiled eggs. My guys could live with a lot of hardships, but food rationing was killing them! The word came down we would soon be served MREs. My guys let out a muted collective groan. It was what it was. Then a convoy made it through. Crisis averted!

The weather got hot. Along with everything else, water became scarce. Then the flies returned. These were the most aggressive species of fly I have ever seen. They were bloodsucking creatures from hell; and fast as lightning. They could land, bite you, and be gone in a tenth of a second. Welts formed even before you rubbed the bite. Flyswatters became a premium item in the trailer parks. If we could have just trained the feral cats to eat them, life would have been better. As soon as the sun went down the flies disappeared, only to reemerge minutes after sunrise. We hated the little bastards.

Around this time, once again with the help of Colonel Sabol, I was able to get ID cards for the team identifying us as DOD employees. Up until now we had nothing that identified us as working on a DOD contract. These common access cards (CAC) allowed us official entry into all the military chow halls, PXs, and other places that had been technically off-limits to us. The CAC assigned each member of the team a government service (GS) rank—anywhere from GS 12 to GS 15. In the military world a rank of GS 15 rates higher than a colonel but below a general. I had gotten a GS 15. The next higher rank is SES 1, reserved for the highest-ranking members of the State Department or other federal agencies. You had to be a very senior member or an ambassador to get that rank. Technically, you were higher ranking than a military general. Somehow the Geek managed to obtain an SES 1 card. I never asked how or why. I was jealous but just laughed knowing that Geek having it might be useful if we ever needed to pull rank on someone. A Blackwater VP came into town and when he found out that Geek had an SES 1 he went nuts as his rating was only GS 14. He wanted me to force Geek to get a card with a lower ranking. Yeah, like that was gonna happened. They worried about the strangest things.

Blackwater's presence in Iraq grew by the day. It now had teams in Fallujah and standby teams in Kuwait waiting for contracts to be signed. It had also been awarded the PSD jobs for several CPA locations outside Baghdad. But everyone still, everybody, wanted to be on The Bremer Detail. We had a pretty good reputation—not by accident!

My phone and e-mail were blowing up with requests from friends, and friends of friends, and from people I had never met, all wishing to join the coveted Bremer team. At this point nearly 80 percent of my main guys had extended through June. I was content, but we still had a few guys rotating in and out. The newer guys tended to be younger, less experienced, and overly anxious to prove themselves. They had huge shoes to fill. A few were decent, but most were relegated to the Green Zone team not the Red Zone team. I still would not put a guy in a position I deemed might weaken the team. A new guy's innocent mistake could get the ambassador, a member of the team, or himself killed. I needed the "A" team with the ambassador and me at all times. Yes, I was selfish. More than a few guys on the team referred to me as the biggest dick in Baghdad. (Why, thank you.) They may have passed the Blackwater train-up and been hired, but that got them there in name only. A guy still had to prove to me and the established team what he could do before I took a chance on him. This was Frank's Rule. Or should I say "Frankwater's Rule."

Bill Miller was now the official RSO in Baghdad. Several more RSOs had entered the country to help him. I had served with one, Charlie Light, in the Marine Corps about twenty years earlier. Light had been a legend back at 2d Recon. He had done a couple of tours in Vietnam, gotten out, and then years later came back in. It was good to see him again.

The State Department sent in an assessment team to evaluate what we were doing and how we were doing it. They wanted to talk to me and get a feel for how we were running the operation with an eye toward giving Blackwater the contract to do the PSD work for the next U.S. ambassador after Ambassador Bremer departed. I called Blackwater and asked them if they wanted me to take the meeting; and if so, how much information to give up. They told me to proceed and try to win the contract. Blackwater HQ mentioned a bonus for me and B-Town if we succeeded.

B-Town and I spent almost twelve hours over the next two days going over our entire operation. Fred P, head of the High-Threat Protection Program for the State Department, asked the questions. It became very clear, very early that Fred knew his stuff. He asked very detailed and very probing questions about every aspect of what we did—from personnel selection to training to operational standards to discipline. He asked about the dog teams, how we integrated the helos into the operation, how the advance team operated, what each person did. He touched on every conceivable subject. Fred was not a typical diplomat. He had been part of many teams operating in high-threat areas and knew what questions to ask. He wanted just the facts.

A few days later the State Department awarded Blackwater the contract for the future ambassador. The company now had a DOD PSD contract and a DS PSD contract. I have to say, the Bremer guys were doing a pretty damn good job. (B-Town and I are still waiting for the bonus checks. Apparently the promise made to us was forgotten, while the guys in Blackwater HQ decided how large *their* bonus checks would be. We heard they were substantial.)

Around this time, we took the ambassador to a meeting near Sadr City. As we left our helo, pilots warned us that our preselected route was not going to work due to a car accident that had backed traffic up for several miles. We detoured to our secondary route only to learn another accident was slowing traffic also on this road. The helos took over as our eyes in the sky to select and direct us to a third route to use to get the ambassador back to the palace. We jumped medians and drove the wrong way down streets, finally getting on a highway that allowed us to move quickly. Unfortunately, on this day, the traffic gods were against us. We ran into yet another accident that slowed traffic to a crawl. By now everyone in Baghdad knew that wherever in the air the Little Birds were, Ambassador Bremer was below. As we crawled along, people in the other vehicles stared at us with looks of bewilderment, hostility, disdain, or happiness. It was odd to see the different reactions of people who were suddenly this close to the de facto president of their country.

The shift leader made the decision to have the guys "run the fenders" to provide extra security to the motorcade. Running the fenders meant that two men from the lead car and two men from the follow car would take positions on foot around the limo and run alongside it as we navigated through the congested area. As the trip had been to Sadr City I had decided we should have one of the SAWs in the follow car in case we were attacked on-site or upon arrival or departure. The SAW weighs about twenty-five pounds, and the ammo adds another five pounds to the load. The temperature hovered around 115 degrees as the guys took their positions. We were in a dicey spot.

Mid Day was assigned to the left front of the limo. As he kept pace, a small truck pulled up alongside our vehicle. The driver snarled and angrily shook his fist. Mid Day moved closer to the vehicle and put himself between the limo and the potential assailant. He waved at the guy to keep moving. The driver reached to his left for something. Mid Day didn't know what he was reaching for. He raised his M-4 up and pointed it at the guy. G-Money was right behind him, and he too aimed his M-4 at the potential bad guy. As quickly as he could the guy sped away and never looked back.

On the right side of the limo Carmine was keeping pace while humping the SAW. If you have never run with a weapon or anything else that heavy in your arms, you have no idea the Herculean effort he was putting forth. In addition to the SAW he was wearing his body armor, Glock pistol, radio, extra ammo for the SAW, and spare pistol magazines. Carmine had been one of the Army Rangers on the "Blackhawk Down" mission. I knew he would never quit, but between the load he was carrying and the heat I was fearful he would become a heat casualty. Behind Carmine ran Jadicus, the team medic. In addition to all his tactical gear he had about fifty pounds of medical gear in a rucksack he carried whenever we were outside the Green Zone. Jad must have had seventy-five pounds of extra stuff strapped to his body while running in the 115-degree heat. As a former SEAL I knew he also would die before he would quit. But the medic was never supposed to be assigned to running the fenders. Apparently when we departed Sadr City, the guys had made a fill-and-flow adjustment that landed Jad in a different position than normal. He never complained, but later I told everyone, "It better never happen again."

We had been running for about fifteen minutes before the helos told us we could hop the median in another three hundred yards and head back against traffic to yet another route they had plotted. We moved to the left lane, and mercifully Drew B (the shift leader) gave the command for the guys to get back in the vehicles. Thank God these guys lived in the gym whenever they could. It paid off on this mission.

As luck would have it, the State Department had one of its teams shadowing us in the convoy to see how we ran the roads. Jumping a median in an armored vehicle takes skill not a lot of drivers possess. It can easily result in the vehicle getting stuck in such a way that the car's undercarriage hangs up on the median with both sets of wheels having limited or no contact with the ground. Getting unstuck requires a series of back-and-forth rocking movements, which take time. Our guys made it over, the DS guys did not. They radioed me and said they were hung up and would meet us back at the palace. Off we went. They came in about fifteen minutes behind us. I had sent the Little Birds back to keep an eye on them. It was the least I could do; they had been part of our convoy, and by extension part of my responsibility. We still had not lost anyone nor had we fired a shot.

Bill Miller had a nearly impossible job. As the new RSO of a start-up embassy he was responsible for integrating the CPA methods into what would become a full-time State Department mission. We were on a DOD contract, so technically we did not fall under his umbrella. That being said, other "non-Bremer" Blackwater guys were going to be part of his world. I did my best to work as closely with Bill as I could. With the news that the new ambassador would be protected by Blackwater, I wanted what we did to be as transparent as possible. I sincerely hoped that the DS guys and Blackwater would learn how each side operated before the transition was made.

Once again we went to the Baghdad city council. The place was the usual beehive of activity. Scores of people knew we were coming as the ambassador's plans had been announced. Due to intel reports we were extremely diligent in how we set up the concentric security rings. Sax double-checked everything. The sniper positions were carefully selected, the dog teams made their runs. Access control areas—parking, the press pool, and arrival and departure sites—were swept. Everyone's ass puckered tight.

As we were departing my phone rang. I recognized the number as one of the intel resources I spoke to regularly. I answer, "Hello."

"Frank, this is Slash. You at your destination?"

"Just leaving."

"Take a different route back. We just intercepted radio traffic about you guys. White van, guys with RPGs looking to ruin your day."

"Roger. Thanks."

An RPG, or rocket-propelled grenade, is designed to kill tanks. It would tear an armored vehicle up with ease and kill everyone inside. There are no armored vehicles, let alone many tanks, that can withstand a direct hit.

The arrival, the meeting, the exit went well. We changed the return route. Ever vigilant, we got back safely, without incident.

I called Slash to tell him we were back. He said the bad guys had gotten stuck in traffic and had missed us by five minutes. Thank God for Baghdad traffic. We had dodged another potential attack. We were good, but luck is also a wonderful friend to have in a war zone.

Blackwater established a team house inside the Green Zone from which they coordinated all the non-Bremer and non-Dirty 30 projects. The team house quickly became a holding pen filled with a cast of men waiting for contracts to be signed so they could begin work. As the AIC for Bremer's detail I had strictly enforced a series of rules designed to ward off unwanted and unfavorable attention. My guys had to wear shirts with collars, no ball caps, no cool-guy thigh holsters, no body armor in the chow hall (unless it was straight from a mission), and when having a drink the men were to lock their weapons in the trailers. Guys on the other gigs had no such prohibitions. Blackwater T-shirts seemed to be mandatory palace wear. Guys walked around with knives strapped to their forearms or lounged around the pool at night wearing Blackwater shirts, their weapons littered around them. It was a nightmare for me.

Every time one of these guys did something stupid, I would get the call. I must have explained a hundred times I was responsible for the Bremer team only, and I was not responsible for any other Blackwater guy. We went to the airport one day to pick someone up. When we got to check-in the guy at the gate said that the "Bremer" guys were already inside. Really? After convincing airport security we were legit, we walked in and found four guys there in combat shorts, ball caps, and sleeveless shirts pretending to be Bremer guys so they could access an area they were not authorized to be in. Brutus tossed them out. One of the guys told Brutus he was going to kick his ass. Too funny. It would have been a very short fight.

Again my phone rang and I heard about the one team, one fight concept from HQ. Again I explained that these new guys were unprofessional and were killing our hard-earned reputation, and that it had to stop. Again Brian B said he would address the issue. He did, but it just further fueled the animosity between The Bremer Detail and the other Blackwater guys. The others continued to drop our name whenever they needed something. That never ended.

Some of these Blackwater team house guys assumed any and all of my assets were automatically also theirs. Most of the either long-retired or fresh-off-active-duty guys had no grasp of the whole concept of private security contracts; of how different contracts with specific resources (like Little Birds and armored vehicles) are paid by separate chunks of tax dollars; or that the resources under one contract could not legally cross over or overlap to another contract. We all may have been "contractors," but very few actually understood contracts. The whole idea of contracts and who was paying for things was completely lost on them. Hacksaw called me one day to ask about the new door gunner training. I had no idea what he was talking about. It seems that some of the new non-Bremer Blackwater guys thought it would be cool to do the door gunner training program. They weren't even part of my team. I quickly killed it. Some wanted me to give them weapons, or get them ID cards that identified them as part of my team.

The requests never stopped. I would come back from a mission and have these guys ask if they could borrow my "hard cars" for a run they were making. I wanted these guys banned from the palace, but that never happened. It took a while, but the stupidity slowed down, though it never completely ended. Unfortunately we had suffered some damage from our non-Bremer brothers, and Blackwater was beginning to be painted as the bad guys by others in the palace. I eventually put the team house off-limits to my guys except for Ken who went over to conduct business or to scrounge. Otherwise if they were there, it was only because I had fired them or they had quit.

We continued to make several Red Zone moves each day. The guys seemed to like the split teams, and everybody was now able to get some decent rest and some quality gym time. And the villa guys were doing a great job. It was one less headache for me.

Then one night I get a call from the guy running the villa. He says he needs to talk to me. It's about 2330 Before I can get there the major in charge of the FAST Company Marines calls me and says he needs to see me ASAP. All I can think of is that one of the villa guys must have gotten into a fight with a FAST company guy. FUCK.

The major is waiting for me in the palace. We shake hands, and he apologizes for what happened. I tell him I am in the dark and have no idea what he was talking about.

Apparently one of the villa guys, Gonzo, had driven to the chow hall to get *mid rats* (midnight rations—late-night snacks) for the guys taking the overnight watch at the villa. When he approached the main gate, he reached down to grab his access pass. At that exact moment a Marine manning a .50 caliber machine gun about twenty feet away had a negligent discharge. The rounds penetrated Gonzo's headrest and went through the other side of the vehicle. No one had been hurt. Gonzo was lucky as hell. Had he been sitting upright his head would have been evaporated. We let him keep the headrest as a memento. I assured the major there were no hard feelings as "Shit happens," and no one was hurt. The young Marine was gone two days later.

Again the frequency of rocket and mortar attacks against the Green Zone increased. The Iraqi population was not happy with things. Muqtada al-Sadr continued to preach to his followers to fight us at every possible opportunity. It was a dangerous time. A mortar attack landed a few hundred yards from the villa and blew out some windows in the ambassador's residence. No one was injured, but it was a stark reminder there were no truly safe places.

With this backdrop, I got a call on 31 March from the team house. A leader on another contract asked if he could use the helos to fly to Fallujah to check on some of his men. I asked why. He said one of his housekeepers had seen a news report on Al Jazeera with film coverage of what she thought were Blackwater guys being murdered. I asked why she thought they were Blackwater guys and was told she recognized one of the guys and the Mitsubishi Pajeros he drove. We were getting ready to take the ambassador out, so I had to decline, but I said I would report it to the RSO. Bill Miller was out of the office, but his second in command, Frank Benevento, was there. I explained the situation to him, and he said he would look into it and get back to me. Frank was a retired NYPD detective who had joined DS. He was a hard man—very funny, very articulate, but tougher than woodpecker lips. I liked him a lot. He had volunteered for every high-threat thing he could. Baghdad was just the place for him. He called me back fifteen minutes later and said that four Americans had been murdered in Fallujah, but he wasn't sure if they were Blackwater guys or not. It was eventually confirmed that they were.

The news went worldwide quickly. The videos were gruesome. My phone was blowing up. They were not Bremer guys. I barely knew one of them and did not know the other three at all. What and why it happened has been debated since that day. My guys were beyond angry. I called a team meeting and told them we all knew this could happen on any day to any of us. We had to stay focused on our mission and on our mission alone. Tempers were running hot. A few hours later I got a heads-up that a few of my guys wanted to take the vehicles out and head up to Fallujah to get some revenge. I walked to the office and saw about ten guys all kitted up getting ready to head out. I gruffly told them to go to bed. I grabbed the car keys and took them with me back to my trailer. The ambassador was working the next day and so were we.

Blackwater, for better or for worse, was now more famous than ever.

APRIL 2004—NAJAF

Post Fallujah we got condolences from everyone we ran into at the palace. Most people still assumed every Blackwater guy in Iraq worked for me. I thanked them and gently explained it was a different contract from ours and we had not been involved in the operation nor knew anything other than what we had seen on the news reports.

My heart felt for the families. These were the first Blackwater guys to get killed in Iraq. Their loss at Fallujah reinforced in my mind just how well the methods we had been using on Bremer's detail were working. Protecting the most-threatened man in the world was a lot more dangerous than protecting convoys transporting infrastructure reconstruction materials. It was not fair to my guys—my team of complete professionals—to have people repeatedly ask them, "What did you do wrong to get four guys killed?" It was truly an apples and oranges comparison, yet we had become the de facto face of Blackwater.

As Easter approached, the ambassador planned a trip back to the United States for a long overdue vacation. I would not be going as I was hoping to sneak away the following month for my daughter Kelli's college graduation. From the day I left on 19 August 2003, I had promised her I would be there, and I had every intention of being there, come hell or high water. We got both.

Najaf, one of the holiest cities in Iraq, was both home to a number of influential Shiite clerics and a hot bed of insurgency.

Imam al-Sistani, one of the most important clerics, wielded tremendous clout from his downtown mosque. Muqtada al-Sadr, whose group was the most troublesome from a security perspective, also had a presence. We had taken the ambassador to Najaf a few months earlier, and it had been an uneventful trip. Just the way we liked.

Now Blackwater had an eight-man PSD team providing security for the head of the new U.S. consular delegation at the CPA compound in Najaf. The coalition's military presence there included small contingents from Spain, El Salvador, and Honduras. I knew a couple of the Blackwater guys who were there—two of them, Goldberg and Tony T, had worked earlier on Bremer's detail. They had good reputations and by all accounts were doing an excellent job up in Najaf.

Recently al-Sadr's local followers had been protesting and creating disturbances, and had everyone inside the CPA compound a little shook up. Calls of "Death to the Americans," were louder than ever, and the Fallujah murders seemed to embolden the insurgents even more. It was getting very tense there.

I got a call on Friday, 2 April, around 2100 hours from the program manager for the Najaf team asking me if we could help them out. He explained to me his guys were hearing rumors of an attack on the grounds the next day. I asked him for the grid coordinates, and as luck would have it, he did not have them. How the hell could I plan a mission without grid coordinates? You can't make this stuff up. A program manager who was asking for help but could not even tell me the exact location of his people was deeply troubling.

I told him to keep me posted if things got ugly. Then I called Hacksaw, and we talked about the feasibility of flying from Baghdad to Najaf. Of course, the first thing he asked for were the grid coordinates. I told him that I hoped to have them the next day. He was concerned about fuel stops, what he would run into on the way to or back from Najaf, and the never-ending inability to communicate on missions with any folks other than our detail. I knew once I engaged Hacksaw he would begin to formulate a plan he thought would work. I checked the ambassador's schedule and saw we had a moderate day scheduled with no Red Zone moves planned. I could not send the helos anywhere if the boss was in the Red Zone. Something told me Saturday would be an interesting day. I called two of my intel guys to see what they had been hearing from their sources. I met one at 2330 hours and the other at 0030. Both said the same thing: there were rumors of potential problems but no sure details. Many times the call to fight went unanswered. Sometimes mob mentality took over and the game was on. I had nothing solid. I slept fitfully.

We picked up the ambassador at the usual 0630 and began our regular routine. The Najaf PM called me and said his guys were reporting sporadic shooting at the CPA compound. I knew that Spanish, Honduran, and El Salvadoran military units were there, so at this point I was not alarmed. A CPA compound taking fire was a pretty normal thing. He called back and said his guys could see a crowd gathering and they were armed with AK-47s and RPGs. Still, I was banking on the coalition military guys to handle a direct assault on the compound. I called Hacksaw. He said he had figured out the logistics of how we could make this thing work if push came to shove. Once again he asked for the grid coordinates. I still did not have them. We continued our normal routine.

My phone rang again, and the Najaf PM told me the attack was under way and the Spanish were refusing to fight. For some reason the Spanish commander thought he could work out some sort of political compromise to the situation. Of course he had no authority to handle anything on the political side. This meant the eight Blackwater guys, a handful of U.S. military—four Marines who happened to have been working on the communications capabilities at the compound plus a handful of U.S Army soldiers—and the El Salvadorans and Hondurans would now be fighting hundreds of guys trying to storm the compound. The bad guys had snipers hiding in the hospital across the street who were firing at the compound as the crowd was moving forward. I went to see the ambassador and told him what the Blackwater guys were reporting. Of course he had already been informed by the head CPA guy in Najaf. I went to the Joint Operations Center (JOC) that was the CPA's military command post to see what the military had planned to support the guys holding off the attackers. They told me there was nothing in the works as of yet. According to their intelligence, nothing was happening. I shared what I was being told by the guys on the ground. They just stared at me.

With visions of the guys in Fallujah burned, dismembered, and hanging from a bridge, I called Hacksaw. We met in the chow hall to discuss our options. Unbeknownst to me Hacksaw had also gotten a call that morning about forty-five minutes earlier from White

Boy asking for help. White Boy, a former SEAL and now the Blackwater team leader on the ground in Najaf, had worked with Hacksaw when they were active-duty military. He had told Hacksaw they were in deep shit. Our meeting took on added significance and meaning—White Boy was not prone to exaggeration.

"Hacksaw, what do you think?"

"Hell, I think we can get there with one fuel stop. But I'm down one pilot. And it would be nice if I knew exactly where we were going."

"I know, I'm supposed to get the grid coordinates later today. How much ammo can we carry in the two helos with two shooters in each?"

"Not as much as they're going to need if it gets ugly."

"Any chance we can fly a single pilot in the third bird?"

"Of course we can, if you authorize it."

"Shit. Thanks for that. What will Blackwater Air say about that?"

"You let me worry about that. Can you get clearance from the JOC for us to go?"

"Hell, no. If we go, it's all on us."

"Great. But those guys need our help."

"I know. I'll keep you posted. We've got to do something. I'm just not sure what, not just yet."

"Hell, Frankwater! That's what we do. We make shit happen. Let's go."

Typical Hacksaw.

The situation was not good. We did not have permission to go, we didn't know exactly where we were going, and what we had planned was somewhat outside the scope, to put it mildly, of Blackwater's contract to protect Ambassador Bremer. Second, if somebody got killed or a helo went down, it was my ass. Third, if the ambassador had to make a Red Zone move, the helos would be off station. There was no way, with the unrest in and around Baghdad, I could put the boss in jeopardy by leaving the palace grounds without air cover.

I got another call from Najaf. The battle was raging full tilt, and the Spanish were still not engaging. The Blackwater guys had assumed positions on a rooftop and were returning fire with all the weapons that they had available. The El Salvadorans and Hondurans were engaged in hand-to-hand combat with the insurgents. This was not good. I went to the ambassador's office again. He saw me and asked what I was getting from the Blackwater guys there on the ground. I told him what I knew. He said he was hearing the same thing. I headed back over to the JOC to see what was being done, and again was told they had no plans.

The Najaf guys called and said they would run out of ammo soon, that there was no way they could hold the compound overnight. To send my guys and my helos to Najaf was a decision that rested totally on my shoulders. I called Ken and told him to meet me ASAP at the front door to the palace. I told him what was going on and that I needed a quick sanity check. Ken told me what he thought, and I made the decision and did what I believed was the right thing.

With only a convention center gig in the Green Zone on the ambassador's schedule and the current situation getting crazier, I felt pretty certain there would be no Red Zone mission. I was between a rock and a hard place. If I asked permission and was denied, we couldn't go. The military was claiming nothing was happening. I could not ask the ambassador to put his day on hold while I did something outside our contract. It was my call, my ass.

I called Hacksaw and told him "We're going." Hacksaw immediately got the pilots and mechanics together and told them the situation. He told them that none of them had to go, that he was looking for volunteers, but that he was going by himself if need be. They all said they were in and told him to shut up and start prepping the Little Birds, and that he was wasting time.

I called Sax and told him what I had planned. He said, "I'm in." I called Ken back and told him to grab a truck, head to the team house to collect as much ammo as he could find, and to meet us at LZ Washington ASAP. I called Travis H and told him to alert the door gunners and head over to LZ Washington. The Najaf PM, who was living at the team house in the Green Zone, would meet us there. Ken and a few others loaded all the ammo they had at the team house into the helos. We had only five pilots, so Hacksaw said he would fly by himself.

I told the guys that if anything happened, to report that I ordered them to go. I heard a chorus of "Fuck you. I volunteered." Five pilots and six shooters headed to Najaf. We saw them off, and I prayed that nothing would go wrong.

Hacksaw's Little Bird was overloaded from the floor to the transmission with ammo and weapons and was so heavy he had to skip the bird off the tarmac three times before he could get it airborne. He barely cleared the blast walls and trees at the end of the LZ by ten feet. Everyone was holding their collective breath as we wondered if he would make it. The other two Little Birds were carrying their standard loads and had no problems.

On the way to Najaf Hacksaw spotted an Apache refueling base. He and the other two Little Birds stopped at the army installation to fuel up. He walked over to where Apache pilots were also refueling; introduced himself, told them what we were doing, and asked for and got updated intel from them. The Apaches were still on standby, doing occasional flyovers, but not engaging any targets. One Apache pilot then told Hacksaw that he and his partner had just been sent to another mission pulling them off the Najaf compound overwatch. He also told Hacksaw that the guys in Najaf were going to need all the help they could get as the situation was bad and getting worse. Because we did not have a radio that would allow us to speak directly to the military aircraft, Hacksaw asked the Apache pilot to radio his teammates and tell them that Blackwater was inbound and not to shoot us down. For some reason we never did get the military frequencies—most likely a security clearance issue. The Little Birds were easy to spot because at this time they were still sporting a very nontactical gloss-white with a blue-and-silver-striped paint job. Even though the Iraqis had no aircraft, our guys took their lives in their hands each time they went up as there was no way for them to communicate with any military assets except via our own CAT MPs; and even that radio traffic had to be relayed through the tactical commander in our lead vehicle. Fortunately we never took friendly fire.

The Apache pilot gave Hacksaw the grid coordinates and

even drew him a map of the battle area on his knee board. Now at least Hacksaw knew where the fighting was taking place and exactly where he had to go. One has to love the brotherhood of combat helo pilots.

As they approached Najaf, with the aid of the Apache pilot's map, Hacksaw could see the crowd and the firefight taking place. Again, we had no ability to talk to the Blackwater guys who were there. Our radios were not compatible with theirs. This was *not* an ideal situation, but we played the cards we had. Hacksaw directed the Little Birds to a spot inside the compound where they could land (not an easy feat as there was not a lot of room) and the pilots, shooters, and two Najaf guys off-loaded the ammo and weapons as quickly as possible and headed to the rooftop.

White Boy met them and briefed them on the situation.

They found a Marine there who had been shot through the chest. Applying combat first aid protocols, they got the bleeding stopped and the decision was made to evacuate him to the main military hospital in Baghdad. Hacksaw again volunteered for the mission. He and one of the shooters loaded the Marine into a Little Bird and took him to the hospital. It was a fifty-minute trip each way between Baghdad and Najaf. This meant that Hacksaw had to fly over the mob again to depart, and then back over the crowd to return. It was not a job for the weakhearted. Not to mention he was flying alone and not in the two-helo tandem formation our protocols stated we were *always* supposed to use. But what was protocol that day? He got the wounded Marine to the hospital, where he underwent surgery, had the bullet removed, and made a full and complete recovery. He was back to full duty in a few weeks with his Purple Heart medal and a few other military awards.

After dropping off the wounded Marine, Hacksaw flew back to LZ Washington to refuel. While he was on the ground one of the Blackwater PMs told him to shut down his machine and to park it. Hacksaw waved to him and told him that he would as soon as the helo cooled down. When the refueling was done, Hacksaw lifted off and flipped the guy the finger. The guy called Hacksaw on the radio to tell him that he would be fired if he did not immediately turn around and come back. Hacksaw told him that he could fire him when, and if, he made it back.

Thoughts raced through my head about the decisions I had made. I decided to rely upon the reasonable man theory. This theory basically states that when a tough decision has to be made and there are conflicting emotions, you remove emotion and simply ask, "What would a reasonable man do?" I had brothers in a life-and-death fight just days after four Americans had been murdered, mutilated, burned, and hanged. I felt then I was making the right decision. I still do.

The combined forces of the Hondurans, the El Salvadorans, the remaining U.S. Marines, and now the two Blackwater teams were keeping the attackers at bay. The CPA folks were safely ensconced in the main building, which was a somewhat hardened structure that afforded a modicum of safety from small-arms fire. But they did not huddle there. During the firefight many of the CPA civilians (men and women) were loading empty M-4 magazines and heroically running them up the stairs to the roof so the Blackwater guys could continue to fight without worrying about reloading. The CPA staff brought the empty magazines back down the stairs for reloading and repeated this action many times throughout the fight. It was truly a group effort during a very perilous time. Had an RPG hit the main building there would have been significant casualties.

After nearly six hours of fighting, things quieted down, and around 2000 I made the decision to have the guys return to Baghdad. We had no serious injuries other than Dave B who had nearly scalped himself when he hit his head on a low door-way as he headed downstairs from the rooftop. Doc Phil patched him up after he got back, and he was good to go. From several different sources I heard casualty reports on the attackers' side. The Shiite militia dead were counted anywhere from fifty to five hundred.

The next morning, we picked the ambassador up at 0630 and began what I had hoped would be a very quiet and relaxing day. We had zero Red Zone missions planned. The ambassador was actually going to spend the entire day in the office. After what had happened the previous day, he had his hands full. Around 1030 I got a call from Najaf. It appeared as though the insurgents were gearing up for a second run at the compound. The guys on the ground were in need of more ammo and any help that we could provide. FUCK.

I called Hacksaw and asked him if he was game for another day in Najaf. His new pilot had arrived, and our protocol called for this to be day one of his training. We talked about Najaf and decided we'd give it a few hours to see what transpired. I called and told them to keep me posted. My biggest concern was their dwindling ammo supply. It's tough to fight when you have no bullets.

Three of the guys who had made the first run to Najaf were rotating out that day. I wished them well and knew none of them would be back. They as much as said so. T-Bone and Dave B were both former Marines and good guys. I would miss them.

Najaf called back again and said things were getting uglier. Sax, Hacksaw, and I huddled and decided to make a second trip down. I had not heard a word from Blackwater headquarters and did not know if they knew what I had done. Hell, I thought I was already going to get executed for yesterday's decision; they couldn't kill me twice.

We met at the LZ, loaded ammo, and off we went once again. This time it was six pilots and six shooters and thousands of rounds of ammo. We flew directly there. I was in Hacksaw's Little Bird with Sax and the new pilot, Jerry. As we approached the compound there was a tremendous explosion. The force hit our helo and blew it for what felt like ten yards directly to the left. I thought we'd been hit by an RPG. Hacksaw yelled into the radio, laughing as he said, "Hang on, boys, I got this."

Hang on? That was a little late. The concussion of the bomb blast nearly blew Sax and me out of the back of the helo. The rear area of a Little Bird is nothing more than a metal floor. No seats, nothing. They are designed that way so you can easily clean out ammo casings, vomit, or blood. Fortunately, our homemade seat belts of carabineers and webbing kept us in. Lady Luck was still on our side.

Have I mentioned the communications issue? As we were flying in unannounced, the Marines had called for an air strike on some bad guys in a building just outside the compound. Our flight path took us over the building, just coincidentally as a JDAM (Joint Direct Attack Munition—a laser-guided bomb dropped by fighter aircraft) hit, penetrated, detonated, and completely destroyed the structure. It begs the question: Did the air strike kill people who would have killed us as we flew in? I'll never know, but I do know that the Iraqi bad guys were not stupid. We had flown in yesterday. They saw how we came in. Things got ugly again today. Were they waiting for us? Who knows? But it did give me a few seconds' pause to reflect upon what the hell we were doing there.

We dropped the ammo from the air directly on the compound's rooftop. One Little Bird hovered a foot or two above the roof and off-load while the other two circled in overwatch positions. Then we switched places. Finally we landed inside the compound and met with White Boy, the team leader for the Blackwater Najaf guys. He thanked us again for coming. I asked for a status report, and he said the insurgent militia were milling around taking random potshots at the compound. Then he shrugged, "But nothing like yesterday."

We went to the roof. The Iraqis were firing off the occasional AK round, but there was no coordinated attack. Nor any mob activity. The Najaf guys were on one roof while we were on another. We had a couple of our guys assume a "countersniper position," but while they watched for enemy activity not much happened. From one roof position an El Salvadoran soldier with a .50 cal sniper rifle would occasionally blast some unlucky militant into the afterlife. An hour so later there was some movement around the compound but it was about five hundred yards away. Our snipers took some shots at them, and they returned fire, but none of us were hit and at that distance with a shortened M-4 I doubt many, if any, of them were hit. [The YouTube video *Blackwater Snipers* was filmed on the roof on Day 2.]

We had a few moments of anxiety when buses suddenly drove in front of the compound. The day before the buses would stop and unload armed militia intent on capturing the compound. Today, none of them stopped. We stayed a couple more hours, then said good-bye and headed back to Baghdad.

Returning to the palace I braced for the fallout. The military was not happy with me. I was not sure how Blackwater was going to react. We had not suffered a casualty, we had medevaced a wounded soldier and provided critical ammunition and support to troops and CPA staff under serious threat, the helos were undamaged, and we had not compromised the security of the ambassador. I truly believed that I had done the right thing

Hacksaw got the first call from Erik Prince asking him to explain why we did what we did, especially the reasoning behind the single pilot flight and the medevac. Hacksaw explained everything we did and why we did it. Apparently the Blackwater Air PM had called Blackwater HQ and had demanded permission to fire Hacksaw that evening. He did not get it. Thank God Mr. Prince was a warrior and patriot first and foremost, and not an admin bitch. He knows that real men make real decisions based upon what needs to be done. Damn protocol! Do the right thing. Especially when lives are at stake. So Hacksaw was safe. I wondered if I was also.

The *Washington Post* carried an article the next day and I was certain that the fallout was not going to be pretty.

Private Guards Repel Attack on U.S. Headquarters
By Dana Priest
Washington Post Staff Writer
Tuesday, April 6, 2004; Page A01

An attack by hundreds of Iraqi militia members on the U.S. government's headquarters in Najaf on Sunday was repulsed not by the U.S. military, but by eight commandos from a private security firm, according to sources familiar with the incident.

Before U.S. reinforcements could arrive, the firm, Blackwater Security Consulting, sent in its own helicopters amid an intense firefight to resupply its commandos with ammunition and to ferry out a wounded Marine, the sources said.

The role of Blackwater's commandos in Sunday's fighting in Najaf illuminates the gray zone between their formal role as bodyguards and the realities of operating in an active war zone. Thousands of armed private security contractors are operating in Iraq in a wide variety of missions and exchanging fire with Iraqis every day, according to informal after-action reports from several companies.

The article went on to describe the fighting, the attack with AK-47s and RPGs, and the defense by our guys and the few Marines and Army troops. It did not mention our Central American allies or their role but did go into the fact that Blackwater commandos were on contract to provide security to the Najaf CPA. The reporter likely did not know that Blackwater had multiple contracts or that our effort was not linked to the Najaf team's contract.

Although sketchy, the report did accurately note the low-ammo situation, the severely wounded Marine, and the lack of timely reinforcements by coalition forces. It then went into the military's official comments, or justifications, delivered by U.S. command spokesman Brigadier General Mark Kimmitt. "On a rooftop yesterday in an-Najaf . . . a small group of American soldiers and coalition soldiers . . . who had just been through about three and a half hours of combat, I looked in their eyes, there was no crisis. They knew what they were here for. . . . They'd lost three wounded. We were sitting there among the bullet shells—the bullet casings—and, frankly, the blood of their comrades, and they were absolutely confident."

The news article concluded by recapping the brutal slaying of the four Blackwater contractors in Fallujah only days prior to the Najaf attack.

Interestingly, after the news of our rescue in Najaf hit the mainstream media, Blackwater experienced a PR coup. People saw that Blackwater would look out for its people. Blackwater in North Carolina, and Ken in the palace were inundated with requests for jobs. When I was not available, people automatically would look for Ken. Somehow word had gotten out that Ken was an executive for Blackwater and that he could help get people on the detail. He fielded many requests from both males and females, military and nonmilitary. Some of the stories were hysterical. Everybody wanted to be part of what we were and what we were building.

We had female military types that promised Ken a night he would never forget if he could get them hired. We had truck drivers who asked if their fathers could get a job as they were badass, hard-assed killers who had served in Vietnam. Active-duty military guys wanted to join as soon as their enlistments were up. Everyone fancied themselves capable of doing the job despite the fact that they really had no idea what we were doing. Trying to explain that we played defense, not offense, was tough to get across. Ken was polite and tried to explain that the decisions were made in North Carolina not in Baghdad. He forwarded many résumés. He did not hire anyone. Nor did he get a Blackwater executive's salary. In fact, since Blackwater didn't view Ken's role in the mission to be as vital as I did, they even tried to cut his pay at one point. They would still bill him to the government at the full daily rate that the contract specified, but he'd be paid less so the company could keep more for the profit margin. I lobbied Mr. Prince directly on this point and managed to keep Ken at the same pay as the rest of the team, but it took a little convincing. Baghdad was dangerous for everybody who served there whether you were in an office or in an armored SUV. Indirect fire and stray bullets do not discriminate. And Ken gave me supreme peace of mind. Because Ken kept the admin wolves at bay I was able to concentrate on the ambassador. Without Ken my life would have sucked way worse than it did.

Monday we were back to the grind: more Red Zone runs, more intel reports coming in, and more planning for future missions. More new guys arrived. I settled back into my zone. If something were going to happen, it would happen quickly. And then nothing happened. Monday came and went.

Tuesday arrived and we worked just as we always did. Some of the guys were pissed at me for not letting them make the Najaf run. I called a team meeting and told the team that I decided the door gunners would go because I thought we would have to fight our way in and out, and that the additional guys I had picked were solid combat vets who had fought in urban environments. It was nothing personal, just a business decision that I had to make. We finished the meeting and my phone rang. I looked at the caller ID. It was Blackwater. I took a deep breath and answered.

"Frank speaking."

"Frank, this is Erik Prince."

"Sir, how are you?"

"I'm good. Just called to tell you that you did a great job with the Najaf decision. Well done. We're all proud of you."

"Thank you, sir."

"I know it wasn't an easy decision, but in light of recent events, I'm glad you did it and I back you 100 percent."

"Thank you, sir."

"Good. Now get back to work and keep doing what you're doing."

"Roger that."

I took another deep breath and realized that I was going to survive to fight another day. I got a few other calls from

Blackwater execs all saying basically the same thing. The only one I did not hear from was our own program manager in Baghdad. Imagine that.

Three new guys arrived. Clutch, a former Army Ranger, and Mongo B (former SEAL—he became Mongo B as we already had a Mongo on the team) fit in immediately. Mongo B went to the advance team. Clutch started on the detail team but eventually became one of the few guys to work as a door gunner and on the advance team as well. Hailing from West Virginia, Clutch had a moderate southern drawl and pretended he was not as smart as he was. He was, by far, one of the smartest guys on the team and one of the best guys I ever met. Since The Bremer Detail I have worked with him throughout the world.

The third was a self-described martial arts guy who came in thumping his chest about being one of the baddest men on the planet. Looking at his hands, you could tell he had spent a lot of time hitting the bag. He went to the Green Zone detail team initially. On his first few runs he was constantly out of position. Arrivals and departures are like a ballet. Everyone has to go to their spots and cover their areas of responsibility. He just couldn't get it right, and as a result he put the ambassador and the team in jeopardy. Drew B was the shift leader and he worked him hard after hours in an attempt to get him dialed in. Strike 1. We wondered how he had made it through the train-up.

On his first Red Zone mission he got into the vehicle and as we exited the Green Zone, he charged (loaded) his M-4 and loaded his Glock. It nearly gave everyone in the vehicle a heart attack. Travis T was driving and wanted to kill him. We carried weapons loaded at all times. The bad guys never gave us a heads-up when they might attack. When we asked why he was unloaded, he responded that he wasn't comfortable with a loaded weapon in the Green Zone. It is a proven fact in high-stress situations such as a gunfight that you lose your fine motor skills and are left only with the ability to perform large muscle movements. That is why we practice, practice, practice—and practice some more. Blackwater trained us with several thousand rounds per person specifically to develop the muscle memory and presence of mind that will save one's life, and the ambassador's, if and when things went bad. If you are not perfectly comfortable with muzzle discipline, trigger control, and the absolute certainty that you can safely handle a weapon under duress, then you have no business carrying one for a living. On the Glock pistol your finger is the safety. If you don't put your finger inside the trigger guard and don't put your finger on the trigger unless you absolutely intend to kill someone, then you won't have any mistakes or any problems. All armed professionals know this. How could you arrive in an active combat zone and not feel comfortable with issued weapons? Drew B counseled him again. Strike 2.

We picked the ambassador up at his usual time and took him to the palace. As we arrived at the palace the team dismounted and took their security positions. Drew B gave the okay. I got out and opened the limo door for the ambassador who began the fifteen-foot walk past the FAST Company Marines into the palace. This was a secure area. Just then the martial artist bursts through the doors and into the palace, raises his M-4 pointing it at several frightened CPA employees, and yells: "All clear."

WTF!? The ambassador looked at me quizzically and shook his head. I said I would take care of it. Room clearing in the palace? I had seen many stupid things up to this point, but this was by far the worst one yet. We had worked long and hard to be the quiet professionals, especially inside the palace. This was totally unacceptable. And, of course, this was more ammo for the anti-Blackwater folks who were working at the palace. I was beyond livid.

Drew B and I huddled. We agreed: strike 3. We collected the martial artist's weapons, told him to pack his bags, and delivered him to the team house. While inspecting his room after his departure we found some frozen "ice knives" that he had made and stored in the freezer compartment of his refrigerator. Apparently, a real ninja can take a frozen knife out in 120-degree heat and shank somebody before it melts or gets soft. You can't make this stuff up.

The beauty of the team house was I could now send a guy who did not make the cut directly there. They had a much larger admin presence and could process guys much more quickly than we could; and I would be rid of them and the responsibility of their potential stupidity. I never felt guilty about it. Blackwater's weakly screened candidates and friends of friends had been giving me gray hair since my arrival in Iraq. These problem children had been landing in my lap. Now the company could deal with some of them for a change.

Attacks were becoming almost daily occurrences on the airport road. It was not a place to be unless you absolutely had to be there. To avoid using the road we began using the Little Birds to transport guys who were rotating out or to ferry in new arrivals. I just was not going to risk losing people unless it was an emergency.

Frank T, the team leader for The Dirty 30, came to me one Saturday afternoon with an urgent request. He was a no-bullshit former SEAL, and a real legend in the Teams. I knew if he was coming to me it was important as hell. On every trip up BIAP, fuel convoys were being destroyed, and fuel was getting scarce for the generators that ran the Green Zone. The Dirty 30 had been ordered by their government agency to get a tanker to the Green Zone using whatever means they could. We talked about the logistics and what and when he would need the Little Birds to run air cover. I agreed. At first he explained the Little Birds were to provide protection for the tanker. I told him we would do it, but only as long as he understood the Little Birds were there to protect the Blackwater guys not the tanker. He smirked at me and said that was what he had hoped to hear but could not say. We scheduled the op for about forty-five minutes later.

As we were getting ready for the mission he got a call on his radio saying one of his teams had been ambushed on BIAP road. The helos were already spinning up, so I sent them to help Frank T's guys. Response time would be three minutes or so. Their car had been blown up, and they were under attack by armed gunmen. Capt. Chaos piloted the lead helo; Hacksaw was in the second Little Bird training a new pilot. As they approached the scene Chaos saw two guys firing at people. He told the door gunners where the targets were located, then banked the bird so they could shoot safely. Carmine and Cowboy were in the lead helo with Carmine on the shooting side. Instantly they recognized Brutus (now back with The Dirty 30) on the ground and in trouble along with his team. Carmine reported they were friendlies, and Capt. Chaos turned and went after the "real" bad guys. The new pilot attempted to get his machine in a position where the shooters could get clean shots at the bad guys. When they were aligned, Hacksaw leaned out of his side of the Little Bird to shoot, but just then the new pilot flew into a flock of pigeons. One of the pigeons bounced off the windscreen and struck Hacksaw in his left lower jaw. The impact knocked his hat off and nearly knocked him out. Even the pigeons were dangerous on BIAP road. Birds 2–Little Birds 0.

The helos stayed in overwatch position while Frank T's guys went out and picked up Brutus and the other survivors. One car destroyed, no one hurt. Luck is an amazing thing. Had I not agreed to the tanker run, the birds would not have been spinning up and the time to get to Brutus would have been significantly longer. Blackwater's body count most likely would have jumped to six. Now Brutus owed me. I had not gotten him killed on our gig and had helped save his ass on another.

The best part of this story is that it morphed into a crazy tale of me commandeering a helo and flying in alone; and of Brutus and his partner grabbing and hanging on to the skids as I flew them to safety. You have to love urban myths. The best ones sound cool as hell and *might* be true. We still laugh hysterically when we hear it.

We arranged for the actual tanker run, but it was scrapped due to an attack on a military convoy farther up BIAP road. The bad guys were getting bolder by the day. Rocket and mortar attacks on the Green Zone continued apace. The insurgents still had not hit the palace or the trailer parks.

With the latest Blackwater near miss the light went on for some of the weaker-minded members of the team that this was for real—as real as it could possibly get, and it was not going to get any better. We were protecting the biggest target, not just in Iraq, but in the world. A few guys came to me and asked to go home. I felt that if they did not want to be there, they should not be. Others volunteered to stay until the announced 30 June departure date of Ambassador Bremer.

Q and his driving team were scheduled to depart at the end of April. I asked them to consider staying on past their rotation date. The decision they made to stay was in no way a difficult one. Q relayed it to me. "The conversation went like this: Me, 'Frank wants us to stay. I'm in.' The others, 'Roger that. If Frankwater wants us to stay, we stay.'" End of conversation.

That's just how we operated. Need something, get something. They came to me and said they would stay until the end of May. Blackwater was not happy. HQ wanted them to leave even earlier than the end of April so they could set up the fledgling Worldwide Personal Protective Security (WPPS) driver training program for the guys who would be protecting the new ambassador. True to their word, Q and the drivers were staying. I was extremely pleased. I later learned that their dedication included passing up $10,000 bonuses to leave.

The last two months were going to be scary as hell. If the last half of March and first half of April were an indicator, we would be earning our money the hard way. I wondered many times why Blackwater would weaken the team for their highest-profile protectee in order to train guys for a lesser-ranking one. It made zero sense to me. If Bremer were to be killed, they would lose the next contract more quickly than they had gotten it in the first place. Business decisions are always tough to make, but the customer and the product have to come first. Blackwater was in this position because of the excellent job we had done up to this point, and now they seemed to lose focus on why they were here in the first place. I needed my best and most experienced guys down the home stretch, not just bodies.

The palace finally got hit by mortars. Two rounds exploded on the chow hall roof. No one was hurt. The workers even managed to clean up the mess in time for chow to be served.

Chaos and craziness seemed to take over the Green Zone. As more and more people came to the war zone, traffic intensified. Tempers got short. More so-called power players arrived to assess the situation and make recommendations. The UN sent over a guy to offer his advice on the continuing turmoil. His PSD team was made up of Air Force OSI (Office of Special Investigations) guys. They wore their disdain for us openly on their sleeves. We were the dirty mercenaries, and they busted our balls at every opportunity.

There is a basic rule in protective operations that states that the highest-ranking protectee at an event has his security team lead the security setup. As Ambassador Bremer was the highest-ranking man in Iraq at the time, we always set things up and used the other PSD teams as support elements. Many times we would deny access into an event to other PSD teams. Once we had the places locked down we did not want any other weapons around us if the shit hit the fan. We never had any real problems until this UN team arrived. The other PSD teams knew we had the right of way and had far greater assets than they did. They also knew their protectee was safe as hell when with Bremer.

At the first Iraqi Governing Council meeting that the UN delegate and his PSD attended, they decided they should be able to park in front of the entrance/exit point. We had arrived first, and unfortunately for them this was not an option. They ordered my guys to move so they could take the spots. I came out and tried to explain to them the reality of the situation. They claimed the UN guy was now the highest-ranking person in Iraq. Really? The UN trumped Ambassador Bremer? The discussion grew heated. I called my MP CAT commander over, told him to arrest them right now and haul them to the brig. The MP was more than happy to do so and called a few of his guys over to assist. As the handcuffs came out the Air Force guys quickly realized this was actually going to happen. They wisely decided this day was not the day for this fight. When we returned to the palace I reported the incident hoping that someone would explain the situation to the UN guys in a way they could understand because apparently my grasp of the English language was not up to their refined and lofty standards.

Later that day I met with the UN lead security guy who was accompanying the UN rep. Bill Miller had already spoken to him and explained the situation and told him that Bremer's guys called the shots. He apologized and said it would never happen again. Problem solved, or so I thought.

The next day we arrive at another IGC meeting, but the UN guys had arrived five minutes earlier than us and had taken over the front of the building. Sax ordered them to move. They refused. Rather than risk having the ambassador witness a scene, Sax (correctly) waited for the ambassador to get inside. We did the arrival, and I went in with the boss. Then I called Q and told him to get the motorcade staged. Travis T walked up to one of their drivers, an Air Force officer, and he asked him to pull out so we could get staged. The guy was about six foot two, 240 pounds (twenty pounds overweight), and must have thought he was a tough guy.

Travis T: "Can you guys pull out so we can get staged?"

Air Force Guy: "Fuck you. I'm not moving."

Travis T: "Really. No need to get pissed off. I'm just following orders. You have to move."

Air Force Guy: "You can go fuck yourself. Who the fuck do you think you Blackwater cocksuckers are?"

Travis T: "This doesn't have to get ugly unless you want it to."

Air Force Guy: "If I get out of this truck, I'm going to kick your little ass."

Travis was about five feet, ten inches and right around 200 pounds. He was also the strongest guy on the team. Three percent body fat, MMA fighter, former U.S. Marine. There were not many guys I would not fight, but the thought of tangling with Travis would make me cry before it started. He was a physical freak. Dunk a basketball, bench 400, squat 600, run a 4.4 40-yard dash. You get the picture.

Travis T: "You open that door and two things are going to happen. One, your clothes are going to get real dirty, and two, your feelings are going to get real hurt."

The guy went to open his door and smash it into Travis. Big mistake. Travis slammed the door shut and bitch-slapped the dude so hard across the face tears welled up in his eyes. He looked at Travis and saw this was going to be a very real thing and quickly drove off. I'm sure the handprint is still visible today.

The Air Force guys were relieved that day, and CID took over the protection. The original CID guys, who had been royal pains in the ass, had departed. Their replacements were top-shelf guys, younger, in great shape and extremely professional. Much easier to work with. We never had another problem with the UN.

A day or two later I got a call from Bill Miller telling me the Air Force wanted to remove the surveillance system that had been installed at the ambassador's residence. It was a very sophisticated system with thermal imaging capabilities, and it allowed the villa guys to keep an eye on everything that was happening around the villa, even at night. It also gave them the ability to zoom in on anything suspicious they wanted to examine. More than a few times the villa guys spotted bad guys setting up mortar emplacements across the Tigris River and were able to alert the military about the impending attack. It was truly a great piece of equipment, but the Air Force was a tad pissed off about the OSI guys getting booted off the UN detail . . . oh well.

Remembering Jim Cawley's advice to call him if I ever needed something, I took it down a notch and got in touch with him at the Secret Service to explain the situation. He said he would take care of it. He talked to the director of Protective Operations, called back, and told me not to worry; the Secret Service had handled the issue. The surveillance system never left. As a matter of fact it even stayed in place for Ambassador Negroponte when he took over from Bremer. The Secret Service was a godsend to us while we were there. Of all the people who truly understood what we were doing, they had the best handle on just how tough it was. Like many others I can never thank them enough—especially Jim Cawley. Jim was always there when I needed him.

With all the additional people now working and driving in and around the palace and the Green Zone, traffic was bad. The Force Protection team, made up of U.S. and coalition military troops in charge of the overall protection of the Green Zone, decided to reroute traffic for security and safety. They blocked off some routes with additional blast walls and opened up streets that had originally been closed. It took us a few days to completely learn the new traffic patterns.

The biggest problem was the heat of the Iraqi spring. Everything in Iraq is covered by a film of what can be best described as talcum-powder-like sand. We called it moondust. Every time you walked anywhere, your shoes or boots would be covered with this dust. That was the reason the ambassador opted to wear his "Bremer boots" in lieu of dress shoes. On the nonpaved areas the dust was about an inch thick. The roads that had been closed for months were thick with this substance. It was slippery as hell, and dangerous until the traffic eventually blew it off. The few times that it rained, water turned the moondust into thick, sticky mud that got into everything.

One day, on a trip to the IGC, the lead car attempted a right-hand turn but the front wheels hit the talcum powder and the Suburban did not respond. The vehicle went straight at and into a twelve-ton blast wall. The driver hit the brakes, but even stopping on this substance was impossible. Fortunately the vehicle was only moving about 5 mph when the collision took place and no one in the vehicle was injured. The air bags didn't even go off.

The ambassador was in the limo and watched as this unfolded. His only comment was,

"Oh, that's not good."

We continued on to the meeting while the lead car backed up and tried to join us. Rather than take any chances with a damaged vehicle I had the driver drop off his team and take the car to the shop to be examined for structural damage. I truly thought there would be no, or minimal, damage. Wrong. The energy of a 10,000-pound vehicle hitting a twelve-ton concrete barrier at 5 mph is apparently greater than I, with my limited physics background, could have guessed. The frame was bent, and the vehicle was totaled. Fortunately, by now the CPA had a large inventory of armored vehicles, and we were able to replace the car the same day with an identical unit. Thank you, Ambassador Kennedy. The damaged vehicle was stripped and used for spare parts.

Q decided to have some fun with the lead car driver and told him that he was pissed and had recommended to me that the driver be fired. He told the driver that I was trying to decide what to do. Later that evening I got a knock on my trailer door. It was the driver apologizing for wrecking the car and saying he fully understood why I was firing him. I told him there was no way it was his fault and that firing him never even crossed my mind. Like more than a few others who had made mistakes, I told him that he had major chips in the Frankwater bank that could be exchanged for an "oh shit" moment. He looked at me like I was crazy. I asked him where the news of his demise was coming from as it certainly had not come from me. He told me that Q had told him he was going to have to pack his gear in the morning. We both realized that Q had set him up, and we laughed like hell. Just another day with the boyz. No one was immune to the daily shenanigans, not even close friends.

The heat was back with full fury. Hacksaw and I had another talk about getting smaller door gunners due to the lift issues associated with the heat. We needed more door gunners as some had rotated out. I called a team meeting and asked for volunteers. Volunteers were numerous, so Hacksaw and I went down the list and chose ten guys to take the course. He would take the top six, and they would belong to him. The course would be run by Hacksaw and Ron "Cat Daddy" Johnson.

Cat Daddy was a former Army Ranger who had been injured during the Grenada invasion. Rather than retire with a medical discharge he volunteered for helicopter flight school. Eventually he became a pilot for the famous TF-160 Night Stalkers. He was a great guy, strong as an ox, tough as nails, and funny as hell. He, Carmine, and Clutch were my Ranger poster children. Ron was killed in action in 2007 while trying to rescue another Blackwater team that had been attacked in Baghdad. He was a warrior of the highest order. His Little Bird was shot down and somehow Ron survived the crash only to be executed—shot in the head—while trying to escape. The militants also stole all his personal items—watch, ID cards, etc. Those of us that knew him were devastated. The other three Blackwater guys on his Little Bird were also killed.

Back in the command post, Ken was going stir-crazy. I liked Ken, but some of the guys did not. A few felt that he thought way too highly of himself for being only the OB (office bitch). Ken had been given several call signs over the months that he'd been with the team—Radar O'Reilly, Christian Slater, OB, and B-Town's all-time favorite, "Habibti," which loosely translated in Arabic means "my beloved girlfriend"—but none of those had stuck.

When Ken wasn't killing people with kindness to get things done he had an acerbic wit, was brutally honest, and didn't take anyone's shit. Hacksaw was not a fan of his. In addition to the business degree that caused Babs to select him as the operations and logistics manager for the CP, Ken had extensive weapons skills from his time assigned to the Special Boat Teams—a lesser-known Naval Special Warfare unit that conducted missions with SEALs and other U.S. Special Operations Forces. Ken had been up with the Ass Monkeys before, flying aerial surveillance and route recon with a camera during familiarization flights. He had even gone up to shoot pictures of post-VBIED damage at the Assassin's Gate for the FBI. Ken wanted to be a door gunner. He had lobbied long and hard to get out of the office. I had previously allowed him to go on some low-key Green Zone advances since he had trained up with the rest of the detail and had been with the team since day one. Some of the air guys apparently didn't like him and didn't want him along, but he still wanted to fly. When we had this tryout, I broached the subject of Ken to Hacksaw. He dismissed the idea immediately. I later called Hacksaw and asked him, as a favor to me, to let Ken try out. Hacksaw was not happy, but out of professional courtesy to me, and against his better judgment, he said to send him over. I thanked him.

The tryout was not easy. The guys had to field strip the SAW, put it back together, clear malfunctions, load, unload, and do it while being timed. Some guys washed out right there. The remainder flew out to an area in the desert outside of Baghdad where targets had been set up. The guys had to shoot a qualification course while the Little Birds went through all the maneuvers they might use while engaging bad guys. They started with the M-4 firing semiautomatic, then moved up to the SAW shooting fully automatic—all while herking and jerking around as if providing fire support in a real situation. It was not easy.

The door gunners finished up around 1600. At 1602 my phone rang. It was Ken. "Frank, we need to talk." This was never good.

"I'm heading to the office now to check the schedule. I'll meet you there."

"Roger."

I asked myself WTF happened.

At 1604 my phone rings again. It was Hacksaw. "Frank, we need to talk NOW."

"Hacksaw, what happened?"

"That motherfucker shot my helicopter." He was livid.

"You're kidding, right?" I could not imagine this was even remotely possible.

"I'm not fucking kidding. We have to put a new blade on it. We barely made it back to the LZ." Fuck me.

"I told you that SOB shouldn't even have been allowed in my birds." He was not happy at all. Just then I see Ken approaching, and I tell Hacksaw to fix the bird.

"Frank, I fucked up. I wanted you to hear it directly from me, not through the rumor mill. I'll understand if you want to offer me window or aisle. I'm sorry. You put it out there for me, and I let you down."

"Yeah, well . . . That is not going to happen. You've been here since the beginning and you have enough chips in the Frankwater bank to cover a fuckup."

"You heard what happened?"

"I did. Shit happens. Nobody was hurt. Take the rest of the day off and relax."

He went back to his trailer embarrassed and feeling like an ass. I met with Sue and we covered the events for the next few days. I went up to our office about an hour later. There were a dozen guys in there howling hysterically. I glance around and saw what was so funny. Someone had made flyers advertising the Johnny Rotors Aerial Gunnery School. The guys could be vicious. Ken handled it well, with some good-natured "Fuck yous," and "Talk shit when you don't get your paycheck, motherfuckers." He was not the first or last guy who had made a mistake.

Hacksaw was still pissed when I saw him at chow. He reminded me how he had been against Ken's tryout. There was nothing I could do but admit he was correct and I had been wrong. I asked him what happened. He said that when the bird banked, Ken didn't adjust his line of fire or let off the trigger quickly enough. One round caught the tip cap, an aluminum end cap at the end of the rotor blade, causing the blade to lose its aerodynamic shape. They landed immediately and inspected the damage. Carl, who was flying the other bird, used a Gerber tool to file off the twisted metal at the end of the rotor blade in order to get it as close to a flying shape as possible so they could limp back to the LZ. The helo was vibrating badly the whole way back as the rotor was now out of its proper shape. While not fatal, if he hadn't let off the trigger and stopped shooting when Hacksaw yelled, "Watch the rotor disc!," it could have been a real disaster. Ken had violated Ass Monkey door gunner rule number one: Never shoot your own aircraft.

Plenty of guys on the team made mistakes, some worse than others—Ken's just happened to cost $20,000 (lots cheaper than the recently totaled Suburban at about $125,000). Not a minimal mistake but far better than losing four men and an entire aircraft.

Luck had saved us again. How much did we have left?

For about a week after this incident the guys added "Johnny Rotors" to Ken's list of call signs; until Carmine walked into the office one day and saw him sitting behind the computer reading or writing one of my e-mails and said, "You know who you look like? Harry Fucking Potter." That stuck for the rest of his days working for The Bremer Detail.

April had been a tough month. Four Blackwater guys had been killed in Fallujah, the Najaf incident had occurred, the country was in turmoil, attacks were rapidly escalating on the BIAP road—and still the ambassador was moving at 100 mph, which meant that we were too. We had two months left. HB, Drew B, Carmine, Mongo, G-Money, Clutch, Hillbilly, Sax, Jadicus, Kenny C, Russ T, Mid Day, Jeremy W, Matt 2 Ts, Doc Phil, Jimmy Dog, Randy Y, Mongo B, Todd G, and a few others were staying through to the end with me. With the country in crisis I wasn't sure that date was still accurate. Our collective fingers were crossed.

Kelli's college graduation was fast approaching. I needed desperately to get the time off. I prayed for a period of relative peace so I could make my move. It never came. Attacks on the military and coalition forces continued unabated. Attacks on the Green Zone rose. Threats against the ambassador went off the charts. My guys were moving at warp speed, and I continued to press them to be perfect each and every day.

I met with the intel guys, the RSO, the military, the CPA leadership, foreign PSD teams, the folks from Strategic Communications (StratComm), and all others who wanted or needed the ambassador. They would come to me to see what they could do to make sure a certain objective they wanted him to do was workable for all of us. It was great show of respect on everyone's part. They knew that the sooner I was involved in a project, the more likely it was to happen, and happen smoothly. This was a far cry from the early days. We were no longer viewed as a nuisance to be tolerated; we were now a part of the process. They also realized that if the ambassador was present, it was also going to be safer for all of them, so it worked both ways. We may have made their lives a little more difficult, but we did bring value-added safety to their events. It's hard to say it was pleasant. That's not the right word. It was tough, but working together was easier for everyone involved, and that made each day seem better.

As a show of appreciation to us the ambassador decided to throw a beer and pizza party for his PSD team. The guys were ecstatic. It meant a lot to the team. We finished up the day around 1400 and took the ambassador to his villa. He had bought about ten cases of beer and forty pizzas for the guys. He also told me he would stay at the villa for the rest of the evening, and to tell the guys to drink up. We were psyched. Since we had the villa security team in place at this time, I told the guys to go put their weapons away and come back in some clean clothes. There was no need for my guys to be carrying weapons while the villa guys had control. Sergeant Major Purdy had taken the SAWs and placed them in strategic locations around the place, and we were quite safe.

About an hour into the party Sue comes over and asks me who the "ragtag guys" are that just arrived outside who were helping themselves to the beer. I went out and saw four Blackwater guys from another contract standing there, drinking beer, wearing dirty T-shirts, body armor, ball caps, and carrying weapons. If this wasn't bad enough, they had grenades hanging off their vests. I asked them what they were doing here, and they replied they had been told the ambassador was throwing a party for Blackwater. I told them that the party was for his PSD team not for Blackwater, and they had to leave. I went back inside and found the sergeant major. I told him to make sure they were gone ASAP. He came back to me and said they were refusing to leave. By now the ambassador's military attaché wanted to know who the vagrants were and why they were in an area restricted to authorized personnel. The hits just kept coming.

I went out and told them, "Get the fuck out of here now!" They were pissed off. Once again I got the one team–one fight speech. They finally left. I was beyond pissed off and embarrassed as hell. What were these guys thinking? To add even more insult to injury, one of these ass clowns was the first guy I had sent home off the detail.

The next day I got forwarded an e-mail from their team leader complaining to Blackwater HQ about my unprofessional behavior. Blackwater HQ wanted an explanation, which I gladly supplied. I could not type fast enough to explain these guys were brain-dead stupid fucks. Then I got a personal e-mail from this guy telling me that he was going to kick my ass the next time he got to Baghdad. I told him I was not hard to find and sent him my phone number and added, "Please call me at your earliest convenience." He never called. Blackwater quickly sent out an e-mail reminding everyone that we were "The Bremer Detail," to stay away from us, and that we had different standards, a different set of protocols, and a completely different mission than any other Blackwater team in Iraq. We were protecting a head of state; they were not. We were the equivalent of the Secret Service in our little part of the world. They were not. No hard feelings. It is what it is.

MAY 2004

Kelli's graduation was in two weeks. I called Brian Mac and asked to see him. We met and I asked his advice on how best to broach the subject of a week away. He looked at me and shook his head. There was no way in hell he thought the ambassador would let me leave. He told me that many others had missed significant events in their lives in pursuit of the mission. Of course, he was correct. What was I thinking? I, myself, had told many of my guys that they could not leave. Who was I kidding? How would it have looked if I had taken off? I decided not to even broach the subject with the ambassador. Brian Mac had a firm grasp on how the boss thought, and right then there was way too much going on to distract anybody from their primary missions. I called Kelli and told her that I had lied; I would not make the graduation. She said she understood. My wife was pissed. In my honor, Kelli wore a Superman T-shirt under her graduation gown and sent me the picture.

As the departure date drew closer Ambassador Bremer and Sue put together a list of all the people he wanted to personally thank before saying good-bye. The list was massive. Included were all the Iraqi diplomats he had worked closely with throughout his year. There were dinners and lunches proposed; office meetings and home visits. I asked Sue if the ambassador could possibly host these good-byes in the palace instead of heading out into the Red Zone. She responded in typical Sue fashion, "Are you fucking kidding me? Once he makes up his mind, that's it."

You had to love Sue.

We went across The 14th of July Bridge to another meeting at Abdul Aziz al-Hakim's house. The scary element: there was really only one way in, and one way out. Darkness set in as we left. A grassy median between split the lanes of the road. Q was driving. As the motorcade picked up speed I noticed a car careening across the median directly toward the limo. I pointed at it as coolly as I could so as not to startle the ambassador. Q nodded, tromped on the gas pedal, and gently but firmly veered to the right, away from the car speeding toward us. He angled the vehicle so that he could slide next to the lead car and let them take the brunt of the explosion. I coolly talked into my microphone, "Eyes left." The follow car saw the threat and moved to intercept. The CAT team commander told his guys to lock in on the target. All this in about two seconds. And then the car just stopped about forty yards from us. Nothing happens. Was it a test to see how we would react? Needless to say there were more than a few ass pucker marks on the seats when we got back to the palace.

During the first week of May a huge car bomb exploded on The 14th of July Bridge. It was detonated at the military checkpoint that stopped vehicles heading close to the Green Zone. Scores of people were killed or injured. It rocked the palace and even broke windows in the ambassador's house almost a half mile away. Another reminder of just how close the enemy was to us at all times.

About this time Osama Bin Laden announced a bounty on the ambassador's head. Bin Laden was offering ten thousand grams of gold to anyone who killed the ambassador. When I told Ambassador Bremer, he remarked that it sounded a little cheap as we were offering $25 million U.S. dollars for him. The ambassador always kept his sense of humor.

Bin Laden entering the bounty game was troubling for us because up to this point he had not made a direct threat against the ambassador. The bad guys had been primarily Iraqis fighting a religious conflict between Sunnis and Shiites seeking control of the country and revenge for past mistreatment. We all knew al-Qaeda was around, but they had not really concerned us. Now they also had our attention.

Slash called and said he had something important. We arranged to meet outside near the smoking area behind the rotunda. He told me that another raid had found more photos of me and other key team members—specifically Sax, Drew B, HB, Mongo, and Q. They also had additional video footage of our arrivals and departures. Damn. These bad guys were good. They were doing their homework and trying to figure out where and how we were vulnerable and the key folks to kill first. Q was on the list because if you killed the limo driver, you had more time to kill the ambassador because the limo would be trapped in the kill zone. Q had studied psychology in college so he always had unique psychological insights into things which many of the rest of us did not. I spent many hours on Dr. Q's couch. In this case he was not amused, but became more wary and watchful.

We had not spotted the surveillance being done on us. This reinforced my belief that members of the press corps were playing both sides of the street. Again I wanted to lock the press out of the ambassador's meetings. Again I was reminded that if an event is not covered, it did not take place. Fuck.

Around this time a different PSD team took their VIP to a meeting at the Ministry of Oil. They had not encountered any issues prior to this and apparently felt that their protectees were not very high on the bad guys' radar. They had gotten into several bad habits. Upon arrival at the ministry, the drivers waited for the PSD team to take the protectee inside, then left their vehicles unattended while they grabbed a coffee or used the bathroom. Unbeknownst to them the bad guys had been watching and had noticed their habits and tendencies.

On this particular day, after heading inside, a person or people approached the unattended vehicles and placed a bomb with a timer under the right-rear seat of the limo. This bomb was directly beneath the VIP. Approximately forty minutes later, and just five minutes away from the Green Zone, the bomb exploded. It instantly killed the VIP. The force of the explosion bent the frame of the armored vehicle, trapping the AIC and the driver inside. Then the gas tank exploded. Teammates watched the AIC and driver frantically trying to get the doors open, only to burn alive. It was another painful lesson to the PSD practitioners. Do not underestimate the bad guys. Do not leave your vehicles unattended. It proved once again that our anally retentive methods worked.

Around this time we also started locking down all the venues to which we brought the ambassador. Once we had established our security perimeter no one else was allowed to enter. And we really meant no one—regardless of rank or prestige. We arrived at the IGC one day at 1100 and set up our security. Around 1130 Jadicus called me on the radio to tell me that one of the Iraqi ministers and his security team had arrived and wanted to enter. The meeting was scheduled for 1100 and that meant no one else was getting in. I asked Jad if the minister had a watch on, and Jad reported that he did. I told Jad to tell him that 1100 meant 1100, not 1130. He had missed the window of opportunity to enter, and he was not getting in. Iraqi time was not our time. Tough shit. Security was security. If they could not get there on time, I was not going to allow the ambassador and my team to be put in danger. It would only take one man with a bomb strapped to his chest arriving late and avoiding the searches to kill the ambassador or a bunch of us. It was not going to happen.

Soccer is Iraq's national sport, and their national team is the pride of their country. Iraqis live and breathe with their team. After the U.S. invasion, one of the major goals of the Iraqi sports foundation was to qualify for, and play in, the Olympics. Ambassador Bremer spent a lot of time and energy trying to help make this dream a reality. We attended quite a few events that supported the soccer team's, and the country's, fervent desire to once again become relevant in the world of soccer.

One morning we took the ambassador to an unrelated event for coalition forces at the Water Palace, and from there the plan was to fly to the National Soccer Stadium. The advance team had gone directly to the stadium and had set up security at the venue. The place was huge. The guys had a difficult time trying to cover all the potential attack positions to make sure that no one could harm the ambassador. The event had been publicized and I was again fearful of the press broadcasting the fact that we would be there. Sometimes I thought the press would much rather cover an assassination, or assassination attempt, than the regularly scheduled event.

We loaded onto the U.S. Army Blackhawks and headed to the stadium. Two Apache escort gunships flew beside us. I was always very happy to see them. By now the ambassador and I had amassed a lot of Blackhawk frequent flier miles. These pilots did a great job.

I tried calling Sax to let him know we were on the way. Our radios were limited in range, and with the noise of the Black-hawks, we both knew our comms would be difficult. I attempted to call him as we got closer, and he tried to reach out to us when he heard the rotor slap. Sax had prearranged for one of his guys to throw a red smoke grenade to indicate to us and the pilots that the site was secure and to land. I briefed the pilot on what to expect. I had on a headset that allowed me to talk to the pilots and to listen to what was going on. When I heard the pilot tell me we were about two minutes out, I tried to get Sax on our radios. No luck. The pilot told me that he saw an American on the desig-nated landing area signaling to him. I told him to wait for the red smoke. The pilot then reported that he saw red smoke. I cleared him to land.

Smoke grenades usually detonate and send out huge plumes of a very dense smoke that the blades of the Blackhawks quickly dissipate. I looked out the side of the Blackhawk and saw very little smoke, but I was not concerned. As we set down and the ambassador stepped out, I could see patches of the field on fire. Like burning, as in a wildfire! In the middle of each fire was a glowing red spot. I advised the ambassador not to step on the red spots, and we walked over to the soccer team and did the event.

Over the radio I now heard the advance guys trying as hard as they could to stifle the laughter that somehow always accompanies an "Oh fuck" moment. It seems as though the advance guy had grabbed a red phosphorous grenade instead of the red smoke grenade. Phosphorous grenades are used to destroy vehicles or buildings. After exploding, they burn hot enough to melt steel. (Somewhere around 4,000 degrees Fahrenheit.) To say the least, they are not typically used to mark LZs as clear. Actually, they are never used for that. And, of course, we had not been issued any red phosphorous grenades. It seemed as though some of my guys had traded some stuff with our British colleagues to improve their load-out kit.

The ceremony ended and we flew back to LZ Washington. No one caught on fire and the field survived. We laughed like hell. There is never a dull moment in the PSD world.

The Iraqis did eventually qualify for the 2004 Olympics. And of course, up to that point, every time they won a game bringing them a step closer to the Games, the celebratory gunfire turned Baghdad into a festival that sounded like the world's biggest firefight. Bullets landing on the trailers sounded like heavy rain. We were very happy for the people; we just wished they used fireworks to celebrate instead of AK-47s.

✿   ✿   ✿

The Governing Council of the Iraqis had a rotational system where each member of the IGC took a month-long turn as acting president. In May the president was Izz al-Din Salim. It was a tough spot for any of these men as they then became the focal point of all resentment and hostility aimed at the embryonic government.

On 17 May 2004, then-acting president Salim was heading into the Green Zone to go to the IGC for the day. As he approached the checkpoint a car filled with explosives was detonated by its driver. The assassination had been carefully planned. The bad guys had done their homework and knew the approximate time Salim would arrive. The blast destroyed the acting president's vehicle, killing him instantly. It was a huge bomb. Other vehicles in the motorcade sustained significant damage, and several of his staff and security team members also suffered injuries.

The ambassador was shaken. Later that day he went to pay his respects to the Salim family. They were in shock, and his surviving staff and security guys were still wearing their blood-splattered clothes. That the murder took place just outside the Green Zone once again reinforced our fear of potential threats to the ambassador every time we went out for a Red Zone mission.

And once again my guys sensed that the rules of the game had changed. The bad guys were doing active surveillance on the targets they wanted, and they were not afraid to act. You can get all the warnings you want, but when it hits this close to home, the warnings take on added significance. Suicide attacks are the hardest to stop. If a person is willing to give his life to kill someone, the elements of pain and death have been removed from the equation. He knows he is going to die. The thought of being shot at holds zero significance. The only goal is to get as close as possible to the target—the ultimate smart bomb!

Ambassador Bremer was the kind of man who shook every hand and posed for every picture that was requested. It made the job for the advance team that much tougher as they set up the concentric rings of security to make sure no evildoers entered the ambassador's space. The detail team went crazy trying to keep people away from the ambassador without him seeing them doing it. It was a kabuki dance of the highest order.

The ambassador's farewell tour got under way. The list of people he would visit was almost finalized and the schedule was being prepared. One afternoon he had scheduled a trip to the Ministry of Oil. Each of the preceding five days a coalition convoy had been attacked after departing the ministry. I did not like the idea of going there at all, especially after the incident two weeks earlier. Neither did my guys. I called one of my intel resources and asked him to meet with me. At the meeting he explained that his group suspected, but could not prove, that a person or people working at the ministry were notifying the bad guys as each convoy departed. The bad guys would then quickly organize an attack based on the direction of travel the convoy took. There were only a few routes that would take you from the ministry back to the Green Zone. It was fairly easy to determine the route and stage an attack.

I met with the ambassador and expressed my concerns. He listened carefully then said that he had to go. I attempted to sway him, but he told me our meeting was over and he turned back to his work.

I met with Sax and told him the boss was going. Sax was not happy at all. We discussed several different strategies about how to make the meeting happen. We could fly the advance team in on the Little Birds, then ferry the ambassador in via the same method. We rejected that idea when we realized that if we were attacked there, we would be trapped. We went over other possibilities and rejected them all. The only way to keep the ambassador safe was to travel the way we always did. Both our assholes puckered at the thought. We were going to earn our money the hard way.

We went to chow and called it our last meal. The ghoulish sense of humor never failed us. If today was the day, we would go out fighting. I sat down, shoved the first chicken nugget in my mouth, and my phone rang. It was Brian Mac telling me that the ambassador needed to see me right now. I dumped my food in the trash can, returned my tray, and headed to the office.

As I walked by Sue mouthed, "Fuckers." I wasn't sure what she was referring to.

The ambassador and Brian were talking as I walked in.

"Sir, you wanted to see me?"

"Frank, are you trying to tell me that I can never go the Ministry of Oil again? Or that it is a bad idea to go today?"

"Sir, it is a bad idea to go today."

"So I can reschedule it for another day?"

"Yes, Sir."

"OK, we're not going. Tell Sue to contact them and reschedule."

"Yes, Sir."

I almost skipped out of the office. When I told Sue, she smiled. Concern over the perils of the farewell tour and over all the people trying to arrange visits for their special interests weighed heavily. The requests seemed endless. People bombarded her with pleas and demands. I did not envy her at all. Each request meant she had to try and shuffle the schedule that had just been finalized an hour before. How she kept her sanity is a miracle.

I called Sax and told him the good news. He asked me if I was going to eat, and I told him I was. We met at the chow hall. The grilled cheese sandwiches and chicken nuggets were particularly tasty on this day.

Up to this point the rocket and mortar attacks occurred almost exclusively at night. Then, late one afternoon while the ambassador was working in the office, a series of explosions shook the palace. Windows creaked under the concussions, but did not break. The guys on duty quickly evacuated the ambassador downstairs to the basement that the Force Protection team deemed the safest place to be while under attack. The guys notified me, and I quickly ran over with a few other guys. We located an office where the ambassador could continue to work uninterrupted. It was not to be. He quickly walked out of the room and began shaking hands and posing for pictures with palace employees also seeking shelter. It was clear that he was unafraid as he made sure that everyone was okay. Bremer was a true leader. It made us crazy, but he was THE MAN, and THE MAN did what the man wanted to do. Our job was to make sure that he was able to. After about thirty minutes, the all clear was sounded. He went directly back to his office and picked up right where he left off.

Sue got me a copy of the almost finalized farewell tour plans. I felt a few of the places were less than appealing. Again I huddled at length with the intel guys to see if they had additional information, then plotted and analyzed the data against the semi-fluid schedule. One of the biggest question marks for me was a proposed dinner with Ayatollah Hussein al-Sadr. The last time we went there the advance team had been attacked on the way back to the palace. I spoke to Sue. She said the ambassador really wanted to go. I asked if we could change it to a lunch. A few days later she confirmed the change to a luncheon meeting. At least we would not be there after nightfall.

One evening we made a trip to Mr. Talabani's house for dinner. The Peshmerga always treated us very well, and the food was outstanding. We enjoyed going there. Their security setup included nearly one hundred men spread out throughout the neighborhood. Nothing could happen without us having a lot of advance notice. We almost relaxed. We departed, and about ten minutes down the road the tactical commander spotted a bunch of gas cans stacked on the left side of the highway—perhaps thirty yards ahead of the convoy. At the same moment the shift leader reported a man with a plunger (detonator) in his hands about fifty yards off the road. The man was repeatedly pressing it. Q shifted right and pulled alongside the lead car, while the follow car pulled in directly behind the lead. The bad guy was getting carpal tunnel syndrome from pressing the detonator on the IED as fast as he was. Fortunately for us the ECMs were working at 100 percent, and they blocked the signal from reaching the explosives.

We reported the incident, and a military explosive ordinance disposal (EOD) team went out and disarmed the bomb. It was a device made from artillery shells designed to detonate on the radio signal of a garage door opener. Once again our tactics prevailed and no one was hurt. We all took a deep breath and laughed at the frustration of the terrorist as his bomb let him down. They were good; we were better.

At this time the State Department attached two agents to the detail. Both were great guys. They were there to watch and learn how we ran the detail on a daily basis so they could manage the switch from Ambassador Bremer to Ambassador Negroponte.

One big change they planned: instead of a Blackwater AIC, the State Department would now have a Diplomatic Security agent in charge of the detail as an AIC. The Blackwater guys would soon be answering and responding to a non-Blackwater boss. The guys were very wary of this switch. They feared another layer of bureaucracy that could slow down the response time to problems. The State Department has some great agents who were former military guys, former cops, etc., but they also had some straight out of college. Most of these younger DS agents had been doing visa investigations a few weeks before. Now they were in a war zone. Some really were not prepared for the realities of combat PSD missions. The smarter ones quickly picked up the nuances of the military jargon and forged great relationships with the PSD operators. Others had a tough time getting used to dealing with our operators. My guys, after having been there for months, were not sure the switch would work. Respect in our world is earned, not awarded via title. I hoped like hell the newly appointed DS AIC understood that he would have to earn their respect first, foremost, and quick as fire. (From all subsequent accounts I've heard most of the DS AICs did, and the working relationship was generally good.)

I was quite proud to learn that I would be the first and only AIC that Blackwater had for a head of state. It had been quite an adventure keeping the highest-ranking man in Iraq safe. But we were not yet finished.

The DS agents came with us on several missions and seemed to like and understand how, and more important, why we were doing certain things. I became good friends with Murph (a former Special Forces guy) who seemed to understand the challenges that awaited the new DS AIC. We would see soon enough. Most of my guys had heard stories of coming pay cuts, and many decided not to stay past the ambassador's departure date. We began arranging exit flights to begin on 1 July, and Blackwater began scrambling to get new guys in-country as quickly as possible. The company's new WPPS (Worldwide Personal Protective Security) training program was under way, and a lot of quality guys were joining up. Being a member of the Blackwater team was *the* place for high-risk security guys. Some had seen the pictures, read the stories, or heard the praise, and they were anxious to be a part of it. This was a blessing and a curse. When you don't know what you don't know, everything seems great. Many of the guys running the training program had worked with and for me, so the new guys coming in got up to speed more quickly. What you can't train for is the heat, the rocket and mortar attacks, and the constant danger. You can simulate the very real Red Zone missions, but practice is never the same as the real thing. There are no time-outs or do-overs. You succeed and live, or you fail and people die.

I could foresee the pay cuts resulting in the new DS AIC finding himself with few experienced guys on his team. I called Blackwater. They wanted to know where the pay-cut rumor was coming from. I told them it was one of the new guys who had also announced that he was best friends with the program manager. He evidently didn't have his facts straight. Blackwater quickly scuttled the pay-cut rumor for any of my current guys. Their pay would continue at the same rate for as long as they stayed in Iraq. A few decided that with no pay cut looming they would remain. Potential crisis averted.

The intel reports were as bleak as ever. The bad guys desperately wanted the ambassador's head before he left. And also ours. By this time there had been more than a few incidents involving other PSD teams, both U.S. and non-U.S., needlessly shooting, injuring, or killing civilians. I called another meeting. "This," I said, "we cannot let happen. If you're scared, you can, and you should, leave now." While protecting the ambassador no team member had been killed, nor had the team killed anyone. We had not fired a shot while keeping the ambassador safe. And would not, unless we were attacked and trapped. Of course every shooting by a PSD team was attributed by the media to Blackwater, and by extension to me. I became very weary of the other Blackwater guys doing stupid shit, and having to explain to people that it had not been by my team. And now it seemed every PSD team shooting, even the non-U.S. and non-Blackwater teams, was also mine.

Colonel Sabol called, and I could tell he was extremely pissed off. I went to his office, and he tossed a couple of ID cards on the table and asked me to explain them. The cards identified the holder as a Blackwater employee with authorization to carry a weapon in the Green Zone. I had never seen them before, and told that to the colonel. It seemed some guys at the team house had dummied up a bunch of ID cards for the local nationals they were employing. They had used the CPA badge as a template, and the IDs looked real as hell. The problem was they were phony as hell. Two local nationals used these cards to attempt to gain access to the Green Zone but had been stopped. The MP on duty saw they were fakes and quickly handcuffed the men and took them into custody. The MP realized that the color coding was wrong. Of course, since it was Blackwater, it landed in my lap. What were these guys thinking? I called Blackwater and again told them they had more than a few guys at the team house who were not doing Blackwater any favors. The leadership elements who were there were not up to the job. It never ended. To this day I do not really know if these issues were actually addressed by Blackwater HQ.

The ambassador's Red Zone missions continued with a fury. We were doing three or four every day. The guys were on the top of their game. The drivers continued to screen other vehicles from the limo, and the MP CAT guys were going as hard as they could to keep us safe. We were a well-oiled machine. No one even got close. I had a tough decision to make as the 30 June departure date approached, and I wasn't sure what to do. I had my Red Zone team, and I had several other guys who had never been into the Red Zone. Did I sit some of my regulars out to let these guys get experience (as they would form the nucleus of the team protecting Ambassador Negroponte), or did I continue to maximize the protection for Ambassador Bremer? It was a tough call to make. Threat reports continued to escalate. I talked with Sax and Drew, and we made the decision that this was not the time to start training new guys. We were in the home stretch and we wanted to win. The newer guys would have to learn on their own. We were not running a training program; we were running a PSD mission.

The ambassador began his farewell tour. These encounters lasted about an hour—shorter than most of the business meetings he had had up to this point. It was bittersweet for the team as we said good-bye to the Iraqi security guys we had met and with whom we had become friends during our many visits to all the various locations. The initial visits had been frosty, but now we were greeted with hugs and chai tea. They had taught us Arabic profanity; we had reciprocated with lessons in American swearing. It was pretty funny. By and large they were good guys doing the same job we were doing. There was professional courtesy on both sides.

JUNE 2004

Blackwater lost another four guys on BIAP road. They were killed as they were making their way back to the team house after a run to the airport. A vehicle sped past their two-car motorcade, stopped a few hundred yards ahead of them, and set up a blocking force. The bad guys opened fire. A second later a second team of bad guys opened up on the cars from the side—a classic L-shaped ambush. One of the survivors had been with us a few months earlier. Condolences again came my way, and once again I explained they were not my guys. They were on a different contract. Eight Blackwater contractors had now been killed in action.

The announcement came that Ayad Allawi would be Iraq's next leader. As a result he became the second-most-threatened man in the country. DOD decided keeping him alive was vitally important, so they assigned him a U.S. military security detail made up of active-duty SEALs. In their former careers as active-duty SEALs or Special Boat Team members, many of my guys had worked with these guys. I made sure we shared any and all information with them. There was the usual military versus contractor distrust, but these guys were professional and the distrust quickly disappeared. Blackwater teams protecting various diplomats, and the SEALs protecting others, would be at many events together over the coming months. There was no room or time for a dick-measuring contest. We realized that when we were together we became a force multiplier for each other.

Bremer's rescheduled lunch with Hussein al-Sadr quickly approached. Again I expressed my concerns to the ambassador, and again he said that he was going. He told me to do whatever I had to do to make the visit happen. I met with Sax. We talked at length about how to keep the ambassador safe. Working on the DOD contract I knew we could request just about any asset I felt necessary to support our mission. Up to this point I had kept requests to a minimum because I knew the assets were in use supporting our ground troops. I didn't want to put our forces in jeopardy. But this time it was different. The Iraqi bad guys had vowed that the ambassador would not live to see 30 June. I was determined to make sure that he did.

Sax did a very thorough map study and selected a route to the ayatollah's house that we had never used before. We decided we needed additional traffic control points at various spots to make sure the motorcade never stopped. We discussed potential choke points and possible attack locations. Then we made a wish list. We checked it several times to make sure it was comprehensive and complete. There was no way I could present a list, get it approved, and then go ask for additional assistance. The initial list had to be correct.

Adding it all up we needed seventeen additional up-armored Humvees with heavy weapons, three Apache gunships, and two F-16 fighter jets. I put in the request and held my breath. A few hours later Brian called and laughed and said that we had been given everything we had asked for. Next we coordinated with the various groups, explaining to each exactly where we would be, the overall plan, and what we needed them to do. As usual, the communication aspect created the most difficulties. The tactical commander was going to have his hands full.

Fortunately for me, the TC at this time was HB. HB held an advanced degree in nuclear physics. He was smart, probably the smartest man on the team. He was also a stud of the highest order, having been a Division One soccer player from the University of Texas. For him handling six radios and remembering who he was talking to would be a walk in the park. Like most others on the team he was incredibly quick witted and sarcastic to the nth degree. His insights and opinions were always valuable to me. Like a few others, once he arrived he never left. A great deal of the team's success is owed to him.

The routes were explained, and positions were assigned. The Humvees would take up positions around potential choke points and block all traffic as we approached so we did not have to stop or even slow down. We wanted smooth sailing. The Apaches would fly off to our flanks to keep an eye out for potential attackers that might be approaching as we moved. The F-16s would fly "top cover," and be on standby to bring the "pain" if we did get attacked. For the first and only time, I told the Little Bird pilots that all three birds would be flying in support at the same time. Each would have two shooters onboard. I wanted the Little Birds as close to the motorcade as I could get them. The idea was to make the bad guys think several times before making an attempt on this day.

Sax and the advance team went out and set up the traffic control points, then went to the ayatollah's house. The dog teams did a complete sweep around the neighborhood looking for explosives devices. Any vehicles parked in the area were checked and were noted as checked. They blocked off the street and prohibited additional vehicles from driving down or parking on the street. The MP CAT guys set up positions around the block and barred entry to areas already swept by the dogs. Sniper teams were deployed. Sax apologized to the al-Sadr team for our disruptions. They told us to do whatever we had to do. They knew their man would also be in immense danger once the ambassador showed up—the safer the ambassador, the safer the ayatollah. We had to work together, and we did.

Sax called and said he was set. I went to the ambassador and relayed that we were ready whenever he was. He grinned and said he would leave in two minutes. The motorcade rolled out of the palace area. We were on our way.

My guys were tense as hell. My guts, too, were tight. I said a little prayer asking for the day to go smoothly. About three hundred yards out my window I could see an Apache flying alongside us. What a beautiful sight! I could hear the Little Birds overhead. The F-16s had been asked to make some low-altitude flyovers to let everyone know they were in the area, and they did so about every thirty minutes. Everything was going according to plan.

We entered the Red Zone and headed to the lunch meeting. Our MP CAT rolled hard. About five minutes before we reached each choke point they coordinated with their brothers and sisters. As we approached each control point the additional MP assets stopped traffic to make sure we could sail though unmolested. It was like clockwork. As we hit the first choke point one of the F-16s buzzed overhead at about three hundred feet. The noise was wonderful. Q and the team had the ECMs working at full capacity. At designated spots and times the driving crew jammed all frequencies. No signal was going to get through if we could help it. We left nothing to chance.

As we rolled it occurred to me we just might survive this mission. Then I thought, we still have a few weeks to go so I told my brain to shut up, concentrate, and quit the idle chatter. We arrived at al-Sadr's house without incident. Everyone involved did exactly what they were supposed to do. I could not have been happier. The ambassador went in, and I went to meet Sax to check on things.

A small crowd gathered at the end of the street. Knowing that the ayatollah's men knew everyone in the area I went over to one I trusted and asked him to come with me to see if these people were local. He walked over with me and assured me that they were from the neighborhood and meant no harm. They were just curious as to what was going on. Even in the USA this would have happened. I told my guys to watch them, but to not be stupid.

The first hour passed. It was hot—like hell hot. The dogs were taking a beating and had to be rotated in out of the air-conditioned vehicles every thirty minutes. The guys were tense and sweating heavily in the heat. Everyone felt the tension. The entire team had locked the street down, staggering themselves at five- to ten-yard intervals. We had complete 360-degree coverage. No one could get the drop on us. With the exception of a few onlookers the area was eerily quiet. That's an attack indicator: when an area is devoid of people, or activity, you had better be ready. Jad, one of our Arabic speakers, had overheard some local nationals talking. He understood them to say that everything was ready. An intel report came in over the net. If it was going to happen, it would be soon. The Little Birds rotated in and out as they had to refuel. The Apaches radioed and said they had to refuel. I asked them to go as fast as they could and held my breath as they headed out. The Apache pilots did me one better. As they left they contacted another pair of Apaches that had been operating in the area and asked them to cover for them while they refueled. And they did. The gods of war were smiling upon us.

The F-16s continued their low flyovers. It was loud. Really LOUD. One hour turned into two. The second hour became the third hour. The longer we were there, the more chances we had to get hit on the way home. Al-Sadr's lead security guy finally came out and said they were finishing up. We hugged and wished each other well, knowing full well that this was probably the last time that we would see each other.

The ambassador came out. We loaded up for the ride home. The same tactics we employed on the way to the event were utilized on the way back, except on a different route. Again I hoped it would be a smooth trip out.

I worried about the advance team, which as usual would be the last to leave. On the last trip they had been attacked on the way home. I had told Sax to get out of there as quickly as possible after we left. I kept waiting for his call that they were moving. After about five minutes out, he called and said they were rolling. So far, so good. Nothing had happened on the trip out or at the arrival and departure. Now we just had to get back to the palace.

The MP CAT teams were taking zero chances. We could smell the finish line. The traffic control points were working perfectly. The Little Birds were right on top of us. I saw the checkpoint for the entrance to the Green Zone, and then we were in. We had made it. Everybody took an audible deep breath. We rolled up to the palace, and the ambassador went to his office. I felt good. As always, the question remained: Did we not have a problem today because of the efforts we put forth, or did nothing happen because nothing was planned? Either way, we had allowed the ambassador to accomplish a key mission. And we got him back safely. Once again, under very trying and difficult circumstances, we had not fired a shot.

Q and his guys departed the next day. I needed new drivers for the last month. Quite frankly, that scared the shit out of me. Instead of slowing down, Ambassador Bremer kept a more frenetic pace. Sue called multiple times each day with new places or meetings someone insisted the ambassador must attend.

"Frank," Sue would say, "Chicken Balls is trying to get Jerry killed again."

I would laugh, then talk to the intel guys and get a pulse reading. More often than not, Sue's instincts were right on. Many of the proposed visits were not feasible in any way, shape, or form. Sue would dismiss them as quickly as she could.

After Q and his team departed, Jadicus came to me and asked if he could become a driver. He had been in the Little Birds, on the detail team, and on the advance team, but he had never driven. He wanted to give it a try. Fortunately by this time I had two additional medics, and after his meritorious service up to this point, I felt that I owed him the chance. I said okay. That evening Jad drove the limo from the palace to the villa—a two-minute move at most. Jad pulled up perfectly. We loaded the ambassador into the vehicle. We began to roll. Jad pulled up the proper distance behind the lead car. Everything was going well. Then Jad missed spotting a speed bump. At the last possible second he jammed the brakes. The vehicle hit the bump hard at about 20 mph, jolted up six inches off the ground, slammed back down. The ambassador groaned. It was a pretty good hit. I got the ambassador into the villa and headed back to the car.

Jad: "Frankwater, I know."

Me: "Hope you enjoyed your driving experience."

Jad just laughed. So did I.

The ambassador continued to visit the Iraqis who had been instrumental in helping achieve all that had been accomplished to this point. Several times each day we made moves into the Red Zone, and each day the threat level seemed to rise. I was tired as hell, and exhaustion infected my Red Zone team. Based upon intel the bad guys were becoming ever more determined to disrupt the scheduled 30 June handover of sovereignty to the new Iraqi leadership.

The ambassador spent a great deal of time with Ayad Allawi. Going to see him meant more interaction with the SEALs who were protecting him. We enjoyed going there. These guys knew they had a very tough job, and we spent a lot of time explaining and telling them the painful lessons we had learned and what we did to address certain issues. They did, in some respects, have an easier road to travel since they had the full backing of the U.S. military and could more easily get whatever assets they felt were necessary to accomplish their mission. And they were not viewed as *dirty mercenary contractors*, as we had been. The threat against their guy, Allawi, was extremely high. Many Iraqi factions had lobbied for others to be chosen. After the handover their lives would get harder as Allawi would become the number one target in Iraq. I did not envy them.

30 June drew closer. I knew that getting the ambassador out safely was going to take a major-league effort on our part. The guys had to be firing on all cylinders on each and every mission. This was not the time for complacency or to be looking for the finish line. We all wanted to go home and see our families, but to do this we had to finish strongly. Exhaustion or not, there was zero time to relax.

Guys began to ask about flight arrangements home, dates they would be leaving, possibly coming back, and all sorts of other issues I knew were important to them, but the questions and requests were driving me crazy. Throw in the fact that Blackwater had sent over a new guy to supervise the new team that would protect Ambassador Negroponte, and my ability to be all things to all people was tested to the extreme.

The two DS agents who had been assigned to us were a great help in reassuring the guys that not much would change. The agents' biggest concern was the loss of institutional knowledge that would occur as all the leadership elements of my team departed. In most cases these guys had been there for six months or more. They were anxious to head home. This meant that the DS guys had to identify and begin to groom the next shift leaders, advance team leaders, and drivers. And they had to do all this while we were running 100 mph around Baghdad. I felt bad that I could not be of more assistance to them.

The guy who would become the Blackwater "detail leader" for the new team made a few runs with us, but he spent more time doing an inventory of what we had. Quite honestly, he would have been better off running with the advance team and learning the job so he could actually supervise what was going on, and not being quite so worried about how many Band-Aids and Blackwater T-shirts we had. He spent days counting things over and over again. Some of my guys who were going to stay decided against it after watching him concentrate on things that were not mission specific. The team was looking at him to be a buffer between them and the State Department. They were hoping that he would be able to cogently explain and defend why we did things a certain way. Instead, he announced (triumphantly) that he had completed the inventory and everything seemed to be in order.

It got worse. Murph came to me and asked if I could stay on for another month to help with the transition. I told him that only Blackwater could make that decision. He said he was going to send them an e-mail and make the request. He copied me on the e-mail to Blackwater HQ. I was exhausted and I hoped that Blackwater would refuse it as my conscience would never have allowed me to leave any of my guys in the lurch, but I really needed some downtime. Blackwater responded that they had full faith in the new guy they had sent over. Murph was not happy. He was in a tough spot, but there was nothing that I could do to help him. The new guy was not winning hearts and minds—not a great beginning for the joint DS/Blackwater team. Fortunately, that would not be my problem.

My problems were centered on continuing to get the ambassador and my team out alive. We had suffered zero casualties and still had not fired a single shot while protecting the boss. We had not killed a single man, woman, or child. I did not want that to change.

Shootings by other PSD teams were making the news every day by now, and all were attributed to the big dog on the block—Blackwater. It was truly annoying; and it affected the new guys who were coming in to replace my guys. Anxiety etched their faces. They knew the learning curve ahead would be steep.

The intel guys continued beating down my energy reserves with their updates. The messages were always the same—*You all are in extreme danger.* I knew it, the team knew it, and the ambassador knew it. We just had to stay focused and take each mission as it came. If we made no mistakes, did our jobs, worked as a team, and stayed on point, we would be okay. It was my job to make sure that happened every day.

Fortunately, with the huge influx of people, the pool parties continued unabated. The State Department folks now had a DJ every night playing music, had karaoke nights, and even sold beer. The women continued to hunt the Blackwater guys with a passion, so the guys did have a few distractions to keep the stress levels down. One day at the chow hall I sat down opposite a lady in her mid-thirties. There had been a mortar attack earlier that evening and she was visibly stressed.

"Brenda, why don't you get out of here and go home to your husband and three kids?"

She reached across the table with her left hand, placed it over my right hand, and smiled at me. "Frank, I'm having sex with more men than I ever thought possible. I may never leave."

"Well, aah, all right then," was all I could mutter. At least she was honest.

We had a couple of boxes of Blackwater T-shirts that were all smalls and mediums. They were a highly prized item, sought after by most everyone in the palace. The guys started handing them out to women they slept with. I'm not sure if the ladies ever figured out why we thought it was so funny when they proudly wore their new shirts to the chow hall. Of course we always wanted to know with whom a woman had earned her shirt.

Brain Mac came to me and said there was a chance we would be departing a little sooner than 30 June. I told him to keep me posted. Everyone from the top down was very concerned about keeping the ambassador alive. The 30 June date was also well known to the bad guys and had become a huge target for them. If they could kill him on that day, it would be a major score. And, inversely, a really bad day for us.

The rocket and mortar attacks against the Green Zone increased in frequency as we got closer to the end. The bad guys were getting more brazen, and hostility oozed from the locals every time we went out with the ambassador. The guys were on edge. Car bombs, suicide bombers, every type of potential attack had been warned against. Each trip seemed to last an eternity. Every time we got back to the Green Zone there was a great sense of relief. We never knew when, or if, today would be our last day; but that was never the point. The point always was the mission. One didn't do this job if he had a strong sense of self-preservation. You couldn't afford that. It has been said that guys who do this type of work don't usually come from happy homes. Maybe. But maybe that's what gives them the mental edge. Like the old samurai warriors, we live each day to the fullest knowing it could be our last day. Yesterday is gone, a fleeting memory. Tomorrow may not come. But today—today is the most important day of our lives. Today is all that counts. Look ahead to tomorrow and you could lose focus on today. Then there will be no tomorrow. When doing a dangerous job like this PSD gig, our teammates become our family. We rely heavily on them and the camaraderie comes to take on added significance. We are there for each other with a single common goal. The people back home have no idea what we are doing or how we are doing it. They don't understand. All they know is that we are not there. On the ground, with our brothers in arms, everything is real. It is as real as it can possibly get. We keep each other grounded and focused.

A line from the Clint Eastwood western movie *The Outlaw Josie Wales* became sort of a mantra, "Whooped 'em again, Josie!"

They never got Clint Eastwood and they still had not gotten us.

Behind the scenes, and known to only a handful of people, the date of 28 June was tentatively selected as the day for the transfer of power to take place. After seventeen months of U.S. rule, Iraq would once again be ruled by an Iraqi, as power passed from Bremer to Allawi. The insurgents did not like Allawi at all. Plans were being made to get the ambassador out as safely as possible, and leaving two days ahead of the publicly announced date was an excellent idea. The bad guys were gearing up for a final run at the ambassador, and we would throw them a curveball. Unfortunately for us, on 27 June a C-130 departing Baghdad airport came under heavy small-arms fire. An AK-47 round managed to pass through a window and strike a DOD civilian employee in the head. He died almost instantly.

The ambassador had always flown out on a C-130. Now the bad guys were shooting at them, perhaps practicing for the ambassador's plane. It was not great news for him, or us. The ambassador, as always, took the news stoically.

My focus now centered on the hours between the transfer of power to the Iraqis and when we got the ambassador to the airport and off the ground. That would be more than enough time for the bad guys to set up positions to fire antiaircraft missiles, RPGs, or small-arms fire at any and all departing C-130s. FUCK.

No one on the team, and only a handful of people on the ambassador's staff, knew we were leaving early. There had been a lot of travel arrangements made for his staff and my team to get seating aboard a C-17 that would fly us to Germany and then on to the United States. Parties were being planned for arrival in the United States on 1 July.

Late on the night of 27 June, Brian Mac called me and said to pack my bags and be ready to go in the morning. The decision was not set in stone, so I told no one. I packed up and tried to keep the fact quiet from everyone. I did not even tell any of my guys. Loose lips still sink ships.

Brian called me at 0800 on the 28 June and said we were definitely leaving. The transfer was to take place at 1000. I stayed behind to finish all the stuff I had to get done before I left. I called the guys and told them that Bremer and I were leaving. Blackwater still did not know. I set it up for Drew B to call them after we had wheels up from the airport. Blackwater did not have to know that we were leaving early. With all the issues at the team house, I did not want to risk letting anyone there know the new plan. I called the new detail leader and asked him to swing by my trailer. When he showed up, I wished him well. All he was worried about was that I gave him the keys to my trailer so he could ensure he did not have a roommate. I gladly gave him the keys and schlepped my gear to the staging area.

Word began to leak out—the transfer of power had taken place. By 1100 when Ambassador Bremer arrived back at the palace, quite a few people were there to say good-bye. I thought the hand shaking and tearful good-byes would never end. The ambassador shook every hand and posed for every picture. Even some of my guys asked for photos with him. He took every picture that was asked of him. To the last day he was approachable and nice to every person who had sacrificed their time and energy to the mission of rebuilding Iraq.

We went to LZ Washington and I took a long look around at what had been home for the last eleven months. It was almost over. Now we just had to get to the airport and fly out. The military sent two Chinooks for the move. There was a lot of baggage and quite a few folks accompanying us to the airport. And, of course, the obligatory press conference and picture taking that would document the departure. We boarded the Chinooks for the trip to the airport. We were so close.

We landed behind two C-130s, and the ambassador made his way to the VIP lounge where he met with a few other people. The press had been placed around the C-130 that had been identified as the one that would take us home. They were behind some stanchions and took pictures as the ambassador and I made our way to the waiting C-130. My guys kept a wary eye on everyone and everything that was going on around us—what we called "head on a swivel." We were so close to success, and we so wanted to make sure nothing happened on the last mission we would do together and with the ambassador. The ambassador waved good-bye and climbed into the plane. I followed. My Bremer detail teammates began making their way back to the VIP lounge to load up and head back to the Green Zone. Their responsibility for Ambassador Bremer had ended. The crew closed the doors and fired up the engines. As the press left the area the ambassador smiled and he and I settled in for what seemed like an eternity. It was a strange feeling being on a C-130 alone with the ambassador. For eleven months there had always been a team around him or his staff and the press—usually anywhere from twenty to forty people. On this day, it was just the two of us.

About fifteen minutes later, after the press had departed, following our prearranged plan the C-130 pilot radioed to a Chinook helo to tell the pilot that the press had departed. Two minutes later the crew chief gave the ambassador and me the all-clear signal, and he began to lower the ramp of the plane. The plane, which was in fact a decoy, had been loaded floor to ceiling with very real supplies destined for another location in Iraq. The ambassador and I proceeded to crawl over the cargo to the back tail ramp. C-130s are large, propeller-driven cargo planes with large tail ramps that can be lowered for ease of loading. This is also the easiest way for personnel to board or deplane. The pilots had parked the decoy plane in such a way that when they lowered the ramp no one could see us get off. After the previous day's shooting that killed a guy on departure, we were taking no chances. Intel reports were coming in as late as our departure to the airport that the militants would shoot the ambassador's plane out of the sky.

The rear door touched the tarmac and we ran about fifty yards to a waiting Chinook. Not only was Ambassador Bremer now without his full Blackwater detail, I was his sole cover, and I was unarmed for the first time since September 2003. Getting arrested in D.C. with a weapon would have been the worst possible way to end the mission! As we jogged across the runway I hoped that the ruse had worked and none of the bad guys had spotted us. I was still nervous. My job was not yet done. We climbed into the Chinook and were greeted by none other than Sue Shea, Colonel Scott Norwood, Brian Mac, and Dan Senor, who were anxiously awaiting our arrival. Everyone was smiling.

After Bremer and I left the C-130, the pilots kept up the pretense by continuing to idle the engines. Once our Chinook lifted off, they shut down the C-130 and deplaned. To this day

I hope that the insurgents who were lying in wait for us stayed in their positions for a few long hours baking in the June sun waiting for a C-130 to take off and fly over their positions so they could do whatever they had planned to do. No C-130s flew that day.

The Chinook quickly took us to another area of the airport where a small U.S. government jet waited for us. Trying to look over both shoulders at the same time, I followed closely behind the ambassador as we boarded the small plane. In a few minutes The Bremer Detail would be over. We boarded and took off without incident. From Baghdad to Amman, Jordan, seemed like an eternity. It was actually ninety minutes. I had asked the pilots to let me know when we were out of Iraqi airspace. When they signaled back to me, I felt a great weight lifted from my shoulders. We had done it. Everyone was smiling and chatting. It felt great. The ambassador, of course, continued to work on the way home. He was a machine to the end.

We landed in Jordan and transferred to a larger jet for the trip to Andrews Air Base. I called Kim and told her that I was safe, that we had done it, and I would be in the United States that night. The flight was surreal. It was the moment I had been trying not to think about because I did not want to lose focus on the mission. I tried to relax but could not. My thoughts went back to my team on the ground. I was hoping they were enjoying a tall cold drink and celebrating what we had accomplished. At that moment, I again reminded myself that we had not lost the ambassador, had not had a member of the team killed or injured, and we had not fired a single shot or killed or injured anyone in the course of our mission. I was satisfied and proud. All the hard work, sleepless nights, and worry had been worth it.

"Whooped 'em again, Josie!"

I was going home.

AFTERWORD

We landed at Andrews Air Force Base, and the U.S. Secret Service met us and took over the security for the ambassador. The threats against him would continue for quite a while. For the Blackwater guys who worked with me, this, in and of itself, was probably the greatest testament to what we had accomplished. We had protected a man who would need the U.S. Secret Service to protect him while he was in the United States, and we had kept him alive in the most dangerous place on Earth at the time. This is fact, not fiction.

Many things have been written about Blackwater in the years that have gone by. Some were good, some were very berating. I want to emphasize that the guys who worked with me were some of the finest professionals, and finest men, I have ever known. They did an excellent job for me. We accomplished our mission. Ambassador Bremer came home alive. In the following years I worked with many of those men, and in some pretty rough places.

I am not in a position to comment about some of the accusations made against the larger Blackwater community. I was not there. I have read the news reports and the books, and I've spoken to some of the guys who were on the ground when some of the incidents took place. What I do want everyone to know and to thoroughly understand is that The Bremer Detail was not involved in any of those incidents. I am extremely proud of the fact that my team of guys never fired a single shot while we were protecting the ambassador. To paint all the guys who worked for Blackwater as mercenary thugs who killed people is beyond irresponsible. My guys did none of that. The OVERWHELMING MAJORITY of the guys who worked for Blackwater did none of that. It is the few who have sullied the patriotism, professionalism, and history of what the rest of us accomplished. We took a nearly impossible situation and made it work.

Erik Prince and Blackwater took on a mission that had never been done before or since. To have a private company protect a head of state in a war zone was a decision that took real balls. If we had failed, Blackwater would have forever been remembered as the company under whose watch Ambassador Bremer was killed. To have a private citizen become the agent-in-charge of a head of state's protection team in a war zone was also unheard of. It had never been done before, and it has not been done since. With all the extra scrutiny that we were under every single day, we would have been quickly replaced if the DOD, the U.S. Secret Service, the State Department, or anyone else felt that we were not up to the job of keeping the ambassador safe, or that we were not behaving or acting in the best interests of the United States.

Failure would have been catastrophic for the United States. To criticize what we did without speaking to any of us, or knowing us, is disrespectful to the highest degree. Do people realize that Blackwater got the contract because there were no federal agencies that could provide adequate protection at that level? Mr. Prince should be applauded for stepping up to the plate and saying that he would take it on. And my team should be too.

The proof that we were extraordinarily successful in what we did, and how we did it, lies in the sole sourcing of the contract that Blackwater got to protect Ambassador Negroponte after Ambassador Bremer departed. This decision was not made lightly by the State Department. I know, as I spent many hours with State Department officials dissecting every aspect of The Bremer Detail.

There was no template for our mission; no doctrine for this type of protection operation; no tactics, techniques, or procedures—commonly referred to in the industry as TTPs—to study and rehearse. We stole ideas and techniques from every resource we could find. We invented new things every day. The guys who worked with me would evaluate what was working and what was not working and we would change accordingly. There were no egos. If it worked, we would use it and we did. If it did not, we discarded it as quickly as we could. The tactics and techniques that we finally established were eventually distilled into a working form and became the basis of what would become the State Department's Worldwide Personal Protection Security (WPPS) program. Our tactics became the curriculum, and our professionalism became the standard. The earliest Blackwater instructors for this program were all guys who had worked for me. They knew what worked and what did not work, and they had the knowledge and the skill sets to teach it and show you why and how it worked.

Leadership is a strange concept. Leaders lead from the front, not from the rear. Monday morning quarterbacks never win games—only the guys who play on Sundays do. I played the game every day for over ten months. I signed up for 30 days and stayed for 313. When I signed on I was going to be one of two Blackwater guys providing a support element to the U.S. Army CID.

Roughly nine days later I was the first and only private citizen AIC to protect a head of state in a war zone. It was an interesting ride. Despite the problems that I have discussed in the preceding narrative, every decision came down to the two basic leadership tenets that I learned in the Marine Corps:

1. Accomplish the mission.
2. Look out for the welfare of your men.

I sent many guys home who were not prepared mentally or physically to be there. I have no hard feelings toward them. They were out of their league. They did not know what they did not know. Blackwater management did the best job they could to keep the pipeline of men flowing, but they were also running a business and sometimes lost sight of what we were actually doing. And the reason was simply—they also did not know what or why we were doing what we were doing. It had never been done before. They should have come over and worked the detail for a period of time. If you have never done something, how can you judge it?

When The Bremer Detail was started there were, in my estimation, perhaps 250 guys in the U.S. private security sector who had the skill set and mental toughness to do the job. Of these 250 there were about 60 working on the Karzai detail in Afghanistan. This left Blackwater with about 190 from which to choose. By the time we left, I probably had somewhere in the vicinity of 130 or so guys who rotated in and out. Ten percent were fired. Ten percent completed one rotation and I sent word back I did not want them back.

So in February 2004 there were approximately 180 of the 250 skilled, private protection guys under contract. By March 2004, between Blackwater, Triple Canopy, Dyne Corps, Aegis, Erinysis, etc., there were nearly 2,000 guys under contract providing PSD services in some capacity. This eventually swelled to more than 5,000. Some were non-US companies, and non-US citizens.

My point is that what we accomplished while on The Bremer Detail apparently seemed easy to some, and the results speak for themselves. We had zero incidents, no one was killed, no one was shot at by my team, and the ambassador got home safe. Other details cannot make this claim even though the threat level we faced was considerably higher and the profile and schedule that Ambassador Bremer kept more arduous.

I have written this to ensure the legacy of fhe Bremer detail, to ensure that the incredible body of work that my team accomplished and things that we did are not diminished, devalued, belittled, or taken for granted.

Before anyone gets the idea that I am somehow being disrespectful to all the guys who followed us, I am not. The problem was not in the people who filled the positions, but in the selection and training phase that failed to deselect those who really weren't cut out for the work. This was a systemic problem for all the companies chasing the contracts. Of all of them, Blackwater did the best job. To fill this many positions so quickly, corners may have been cut. When money becomes the overriding factor in chasing contracts without realizing the extreme difficulties of the job, there are bound to be problems. Unfortunately, in a war zone, these problems can result in catastrophic incidents. I cannot reiterate enough, there was no template or handbook written on how to perform what eventually became *Combat PSD* protection operations. You had to learn by doing it. You had to see what was happening and react accordingly. Overreact and innocent people might be killed. Underreact and you or your people got waxed. The sandbox was an unforgiving classroom. You could make all the plans you wanted, but when you walked out the door, the plan changed. The bad guys didn't read our plans; they did what they wanted, when they wanted. They had formulated their plan based on the surveillance they had done on us. We reacted to their actions. They played offense, and we played defense.

The keys to a proper attack or ambush are based upon the following three principles:

1. Surprise
2. Speed
3. Violence of action

The bad guys pick the time, the place, and the weapons they believe will give them the greatest possible means to succeed. Action is always faster than reaction. Training fundamentals had to emphasize core, automatic reactions that increase one's chances of survival. During an attack there is no time to think.

All new guys have a reaction lag time. They may not immediately realize what is happening as bombs go off or bullets whiz past their heads. This was a big reason why each time that my experienced guys rotated out, the guys who stayed behind were nervous about the new guys who came in. Experience cannot be taught. Experience is earned one day at a time. Seeing and knowing what is happening and reacting accordingly is learned— mentally and physically. The longer a team works together the more they trust one another and the better they get at the job they are doing.

There were a lot of guys who came in and did an excellent job. Unfortunately, other guys should have never been in Iraq. And, as seemingly always, negatives got more press coverage than positives.

Blackwater eventually had forty-three guys killed while doing their jobs. None of them were Bremer detail guys.

Coming home after 313 days running the roads in Baghdad was tough. Not just for me, but for all the guys. The transition from looking for threats everywhere to being a *normal* citizen was not easy. Going to bed and waiting for mortars and rockets to land, driving down the road not letting anyone pass you, driving as fast as you can, waiting for the trash in the road to explode, and waiting for ambushes at every intersection is not something that is easy to let go.

The families of the guys who spent months over there with me had a real adjustment period as their men tried to integrate back into a civilized society. We had missed many events in the lives of our families—birthdays, funerals, weddings, graduations, sports events—that can never be made up. We missed them, but we had had to concentrate on each minute of each day in the sandbox. The real world had ceased to exist for us. We had left the real world one day, and returned what seemed like the very next, as if our homes had existed in a state of suspended animation. We picked up right where we had left off and expected that everything would be the same. Nothing was the same. We were not the same, nor were our families. Resentments and misunderstandings stirred in all parties involved.

As contractors there were no support systems in place for us; no Veterans Administration to help the guys or their families get back to some semblance of normalcy. We became the forgotten men and women who helped the country. The media ridiculed us and painted us as less than honorable people who went over there solely, as in the case of the PSD teams, to quench our thirst to maim or kill people, and make ungodly amounts of money leaching off the American taxpayer at the expense of the war fighters with whom we shared the battle space. Some in the media claimed we had no morals or moral culpability, that we were cowboys with guns running amuck and running roughshod over anyone who got in our way. As in the military, there will always be the 2 percent who make mistakes and ruin the reputations of the other 98 percent. Just once I would like to see the media applaud the sacrifices the 98 percent who supported two wars and fought thousands of miles from our home shores. It will probably never happen. Contractors are a disposable item. Use them, then trash them. Cash and carry with no long-term career prospects.

The toll on the families was tremendous. Especially after the media began to portray us as worse than the bad guys. Many guys wound up in divorce court. I did. The fact that the "real" bad guys were trying to blow us up almost every day has been glossed over and the stories of the incidents where contractors crossed the line were endlessly repeated. Wives looked at their husbands and questioned whether or not they had murdered people. Children wondered if Dad was one of "them." All I can say to the families of the guys who worked for me is, "We were not 'them.'"

Since The Bremer Detail ended I have met or heard of quite a few people who claimed to have been with us yet never were. I even ran into a guy who claimed he had been the AIC! More disturbing has been the claim by some that they held leadership positions when they never did. In an attempt to set the record straight, the guys who held high-level leadership positions are listed below:

Ops/Support: Ken H, DT, RB, Peter F, Russ T
Medics: Doc Jones, Doc Phil, Jadicus, Dufop
Drivers : Q, Travis T, FB, Larrycade, Scott S, JD (Chief)
    W, Gino N, Dorian A, Bama, WW, Dan B
Tactical Commander: HB, Riceman, Tony T, Mongo,
    Carmine
Shift Leader: Drew B, Bird, Riceman, Mongo, BV, MP

Advance Team Leader: Sax, Scotty H, B-Town
Door Gunner Team Leaders: Cowboy John Hall, Dave
    Bradfield, BV
AIC: Frank Gallagher

A few guys may have held a leadership slot for a day when someone was sick, but the guys listed above were the leadership members of The Bremer Detail team.

I want to thank several people publicly for helping us do our jobs. For the most part I have kept their names out of the details, but they deserve a mention and have my undying respect and gratitude. They worked as hard as we did in their assignments and took the same risks we did. I know I probably pissed a lot of them off a time or ten, but their efforts and sacrifices were very much appreciated by me and the team. Thank you.

This list is in alphabetical order.

Thomas Basile
Maj. Becket, USMC
Dave Bennet
Lt. Col. Pat Carroll, USMC
Scott Carpenter
Jill Copenhaver
Ken Curley
Capt. Liesel Davenport, USAF
Gregg Edgar

Matt Fuller
Robert Goodwin
Don Hamilton
Heather Hopkins
Gordan James
Ambassador Richard Jones
Maj. Kaufman, U.S. Army
Lydia Khalil
Ali Khedery
Sharifah Maston
Julia Nesheiwat
Susan Phelan
Col. Dennis Sabol, USMC
Carrie Schneider
Traci Scott
Scott Sforza
Suzann Shaffrath
Dale Sharagaso, USAF
Jim Steele
Christina Estrada Teczar
Olivia Troy
Kristen Whiting
Molly Wilkinson
Jared Young
Alex Zemek

The guys who volunteered to go over to Iraq and perform this mission are all worthy of great respect. Many guys did one rotation and never came back. Some did not come back because I did not want them back, and some because it was just too stressful for the man or his family. The guys who did a rotation and came back despite the knowledge that they were taking great personal risks are worthy of mention. Below are the guys who did at least 150 days in Iraq. These 150 days meant they made at least five hundred Red Zone motorcade movements while protecting Ambassador Bremer.

The Bremer Detail Hall of Fame:

Phil Abdow
Monti Anderson
Dan Bauscher
Matt Botvinis
Drew Bowman
Hart Brown
Mark Brynick
Faron Burcker
Steve Chilton
Billy Connors
Ken Correll
Dave Diemer
Peter Farrell
Kwame Fisher
Todd Gillis
Jimmy Griffin
John Hall
Ken Herbert

Gavin Horne
Ron Johnson
Steve Just
Carl Magee
Jad Muntasser
Gino Najiola
Stuart Rice
Eric Saxon
Ryan Sharock
Mike Soppelsa
Travis Titus
Russell Todd
Mark Walker
JD Williamson
Jeremy Woelfer
Randy Yonker

ACKNOWLEDGMENTS

Thanks to Ambassador L. Paul Bremer. He was the hardest-working man in Baghdad. He was also the best protectee I have ever had the privilege of working with. Despite all the risks and challenges, he let us do our job while we made sure that he could do his.

Sue Shea, none of us will ever forget you. Thanks for all your help while we were there.

I must also offer my thanks to Erik Prince for having the guts to take on this mission and having the trust and confidence in us to accomplish it. It was neither easy nor smooth sailing, but we did it. Mr. Prince was a great man to work for. He has my eternal respect. As does Brian Berrey for first calling me, hiring me, and looking out for me. He also offered sage advice and served as a great sounding board when the seas got rough.

Many thanks to the guys who were on the mission with me—we did it. Especially the guys who helped refresh my memory of some events and took the time to review the book to make sure that it is correct. Steve "B-Town" Just, Ken "Harry Potter"

Herbert, John "Cowboy" Hall, Steve "Hacksaw" Chilton, Kwame "Q" Fisher, Ryan "Geek" Sharack, Dave "Carmine" Diemer, Jad "Jadicus" Muntasser, Gavin "G-Money" Horne, Eric Saxon, and John "Brutus" Buffin—thanks for the reviews and revisions. Many may (and some will) question the account, but the truth is here.

Special thanks also to my sister-in-law, Jennifer Adnet Gallagher; Tony Scotti, the godfather of security driving; Joe Autera; Geoff Fowler; Mike Marcel; Pete Porrello; Ed Castillo; Matt Marshal; and the many others who kept me on track.

Mary K. Duke—thanks for all the help!

John Del Vecchio—what can I say? Your help in cleaning this up was a lifesaver. Thank you!

And to my daughters, Kelli and Katherine, as they most likely had it the roughest of all as they followed the news and saw what was being reported—though often it was not the truth. Kids who have parents working in a war zone never know when or if their parents will be home. It could not have been easy. But, at least in my case, they knew that the United States of America is our country and as citizens, we do what needs to be done to support our way of life. If the country needs you, you do what you can. Love you both! Thanks.

ABOUT THE AUTHORS

Frank G. Gallagher has over twenty-five years of international experience providing personal protection, intelligence gathering, counterterrorism operations, surveillance detection, threat analysis, and security training in both the private security sector and the U.S. military.

Mr. Gallagher is a U.S. Marine, having served from 1978 to 1982. During this period he was a member of 2d Reconnaissance Battalion. His experience as a special warfare operator included duties such as intelligence gathering, dive operations, surveillance detection, close quarters battle (CQB), small unit tactics, and training.

After leaving the Corps, he served as the director of security for former U.S. Secretary of State Dr. Henry A. Kissinger. In that role Mr. Gallagher was responsible for the public and private, domestic and international safety and security of Dr. and Mrs. Kissinger. He coordinated the Kissingers' travel plans in liaison with local, federal, and international law-enforcement officials. He was also responsible for the security of multiple offices and residences, as well as the recruiting and training of members of the PSD.

Following that assignment Frank Gallagher worked for International Business Resources (IBR) where he was responsible for the creation, training, and outfitting of both the CBR (Chemical, Biological, and Radiological) and Hostile Environment Training programs for clients with personnel traveling to high-threat areas. He also conducted international security surveys for multinational clients to ensure adherence to acceptable risk-management standards.

Mr. Gallagher's most memorable assignment was as the agent-in-charge (AIC) of Ambassador L. Paul Bremer's security detail in Iraq, where he was responsible for the day-to-day safety and security of the presidential envoy who had been tasked with overseeing the rebuilding of the country. Mr. Gallagher designed and supervised the motorcade operations, CAT operations, foot formations, surveillance detection, and helicopter support procedures that helped make the mission a success.

After The Bremer Detail, Frank served Blackwater Security as the lead instructor for its protective service details (PSD) portion of the State Department's Worldwide Personal Protective Services (WPPS) High-Threat Protection training program.

Frank Gallagher returned to Iraq in September 2004 and worked for the Counterterrorism Special Operations Forces under DOD as the deputy program manager for the Bureau of Diplomatic Protection responsible for training the Iraqi PSD teams now protecting Iraq's leadership.

In 2006 he worked for the U.S. Department of State's

Anti-Terrorism Assistance (ATA) Program where he trained foreign protection agents in VIP protection and taught VIPP-TST (tactical support team) courses. He also helped to rewrite the Protecting National Leaders (PNL) course and is recognized by the U.S. Department of State as an expert on this subject matter.

Frank is currently the executive vice president of Amyntor Group, LLC, an international security services and consulting firm serving government, corporate, and VIP clients.

John M. Del Vecchio is the author of the bestselling *The 13th Valley*, along with other books on the war in Southeast Asia and on the veteran homecoming experience. He was drafted in 1969 shortly after graduating from Lafayette College with a bachelor's degree in psychology. In 1970 he volunteered for Vietnam where he served as a combat correspondent for the 101st Airborne Division (Airmobile). In 1971 he was awarded a Bronze Star for Heroism in Ground Combat. His books in addition to *The 13th Valley* include *For the Sake of All Living Things*, *Carry Me Home*, and *Darkness Falls*. *The 13th Valley* was a million-plus-copy bestseller about which the *New York Times* book review said, "There have been a number of excellent books about Vietnam, but none has managed to communicate in such detail the day-to-day pain, discomfort, frustration and exhilaration of the American military experience in Vietnam." Del Vecchio's books have been translated into four languages and published worldwide.

CHARLIE FOXTROT
BOOKS

Charlie Foxtrot Entertainment, LLC (CFE), and its sister company, Charlie Foxtrot Books, LLC (CFB), are military-based entertainment companies that are "Inspired by Heroes." CFE and CFB are engaged in the business of financing, producing, and licensing movies, documentaries, books, graphic novels, video games, music, and merchandise from their library of currently owned and to-be-acquired military-oriented intellectual properties. Charlie Foxtrot's bestselling books and critically acclaimed graphic novels provide a base for the development of its film and TV productions. The companies take great pride in the fact that all members are veterans of the US military. This provides the Charlie Foxtrot companies with unique and authentic insights few others achieve. Please visit the websites below for more information about the companies and their principles.

FIND OUT MORE AT
WWW.CHARLIEFOXTROTFILMS.COM
AND WWW.CHARLIEFOXTROTBOOKS.COM

Charlie Foxtrot Books is one of a select group of publishing partners of Open Road Integrated Media, Inc.

OPEN ROAD

INTEGRATED MEDIA

Open Road Integrated Media is a digital publisher and multimedia content company. Open Road creates connections between authors and their audiences by marketing its ebooks through a new proprietary online platform, which uses premium video content and social media.

CPSIA information can be obtained
at www.ICGtesting.com
Printed in the USA
BVOW08*0902201117
500904BV00008B/73/P